HEROIC ANIMALS

CORPORAL WOJTEK

SUPPLIES THE TROOPS

HEROIC BEAR OF WORLD WAR II

BY **BRUCE BERGLUND**   ILLUSTRATED BY **DOLO OKĘCKI**

CAPSTONE PRESS
a capstone imprint

Published by Capstone Press, an imprint of Capstone.
1710 Roe Crest Drive, North Mankato, Minnesota 56003
capstonepub.com

Library of Congress Cataloging-in-Publication Data
is available on the Library of Congress website.

ISBN: 9781669057734 (hardcover)
ISBN: 9781669057895 (paperback)
ISBN: 9781669057901 (ebook PDF)

Summary:
During World War II, a group of homesick Polish soldiers took in an orphaned bear cub and named him Wojtek. As the bear cub grew, he became friends with the soldiers, lifting their spirits as he learned to imitate them around camp. Later, Wojtek was helpful by carrying many heavy shells during a large battle in Italy. Learn how Wojtek showed his courage in battle and earned the rank of Corporal during history's biggest war.

Editorial Credits
Editor: Aaron Sautter; Designer: Elyse White; Media Researcher: Rebekah Hubstenberger: Production Specialist: Whitney Schaefer

Image Credit
Alamy: The Picture Art Collection, 29

All internet sites appearing in back matter were available and accurate when this book was sent to press.

Direct quotes appear in ***bold, italicized*** text on the following pages:
Pages 10, 27, 28 (bottom panel): Orr, Aileen. *Wojtek the Bear: Polish War Hero*. Edinburgh, Scotland: Birlinn, 2014.

Page 16: "Private Wojtek: The Bear Who Became a Soldier," essay by Duane Schultz. https://duaneschultz.com/wp-content/uploads/Private-Wojtek-PDF.pdf Accessed February, 2023.

Page 28: "Story of Poland's 'Soldier Bear' Wojtek Turned into Film," by Martin Vennard, BBC World Service, November 16, 2011, https://www.bbc.com/news/world-europe-15736812.

Printed and bound in China. PO 5593

TABLE OF CONTENTS

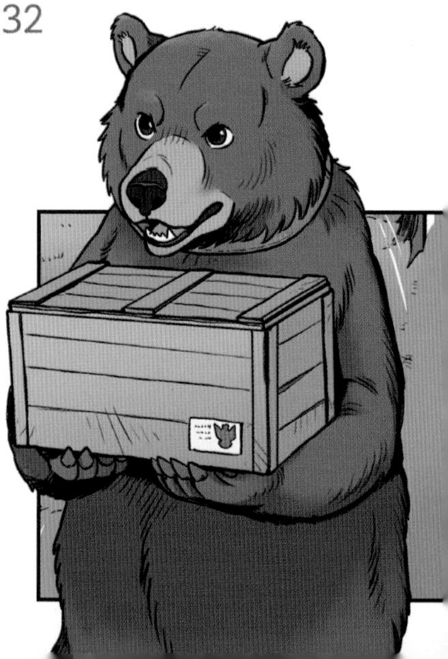

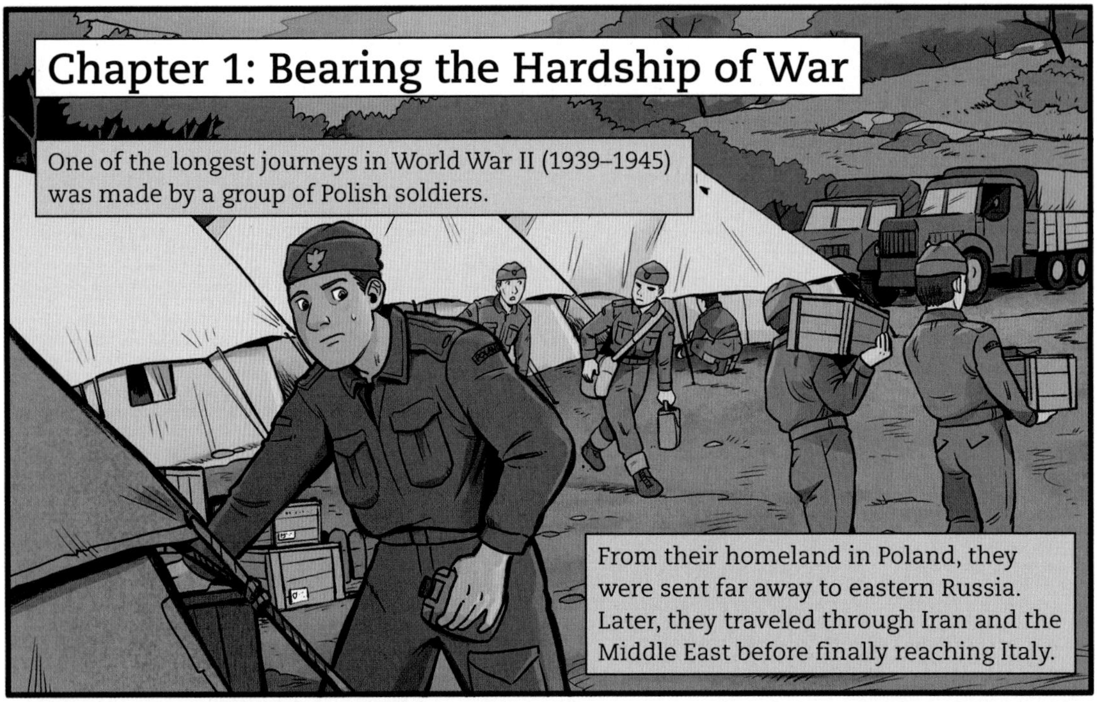
Chapter 1: Bearing the Hardship of War
One of the longest journeys in World War II (1939–1945) was made by a group of Polish soldiers.
From their homeland in Poland, they were sent far away to eastern Russia. Later, they traveled through Iran and the Middle East before finally reaching Italy.

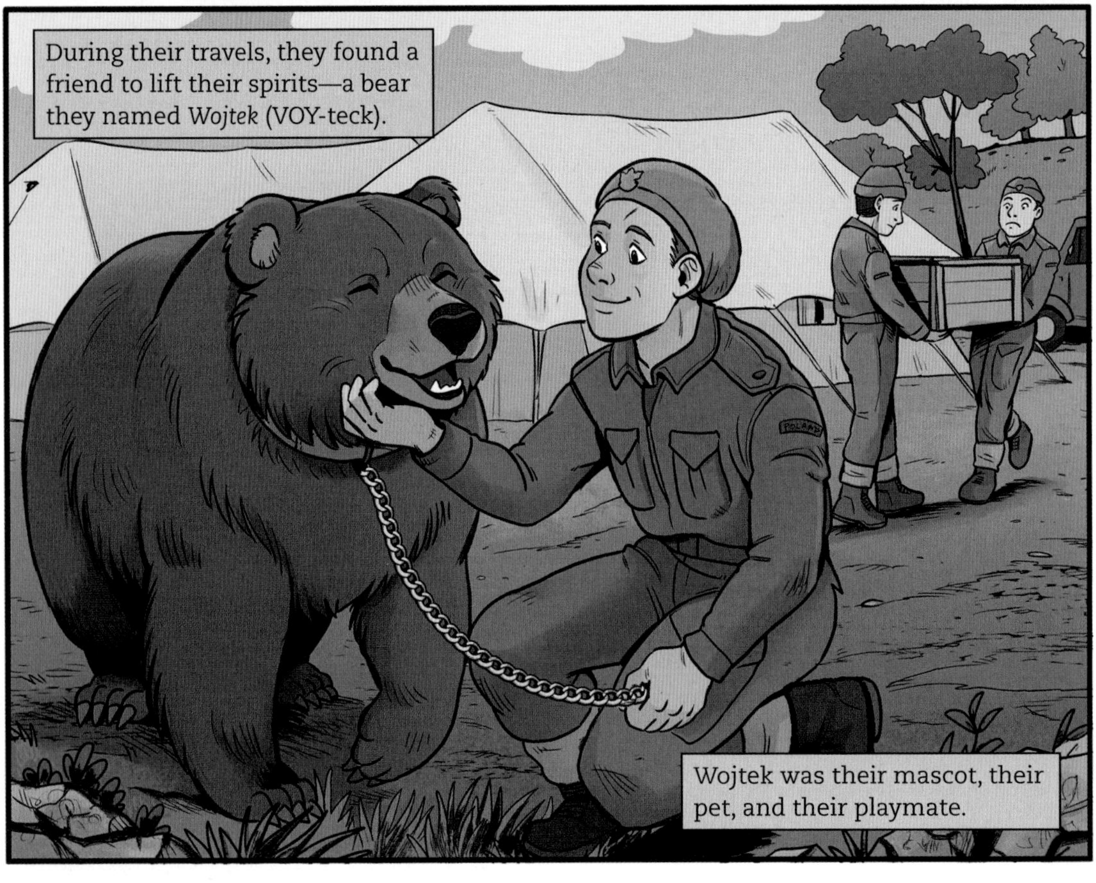
During their travels, they found a friend to lift their spirits—a bear they named *Wojtek* (VOY-teck).
Wojtek was their mascot, their pet, and their playmate.

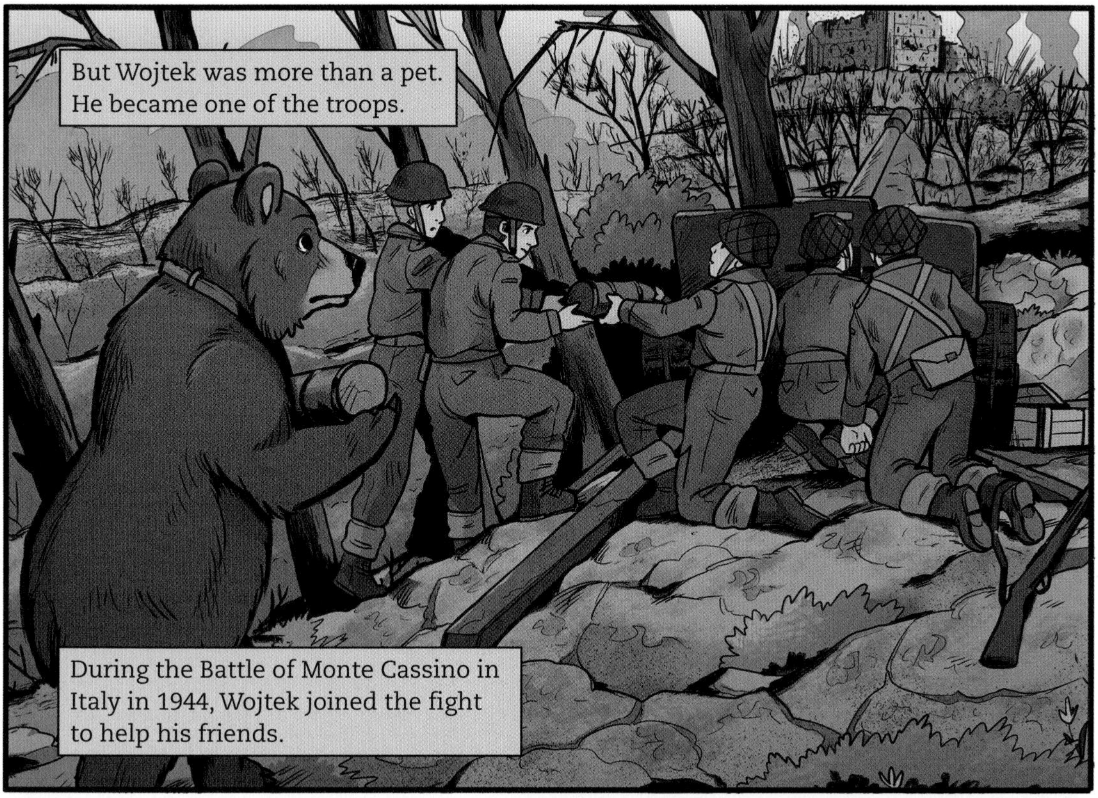
But Wojtek was more than a pet. He became one of the troops.
During the Battle of Monte Cassino in Italy in 1944, Wojtek joined the fight to help his friends.

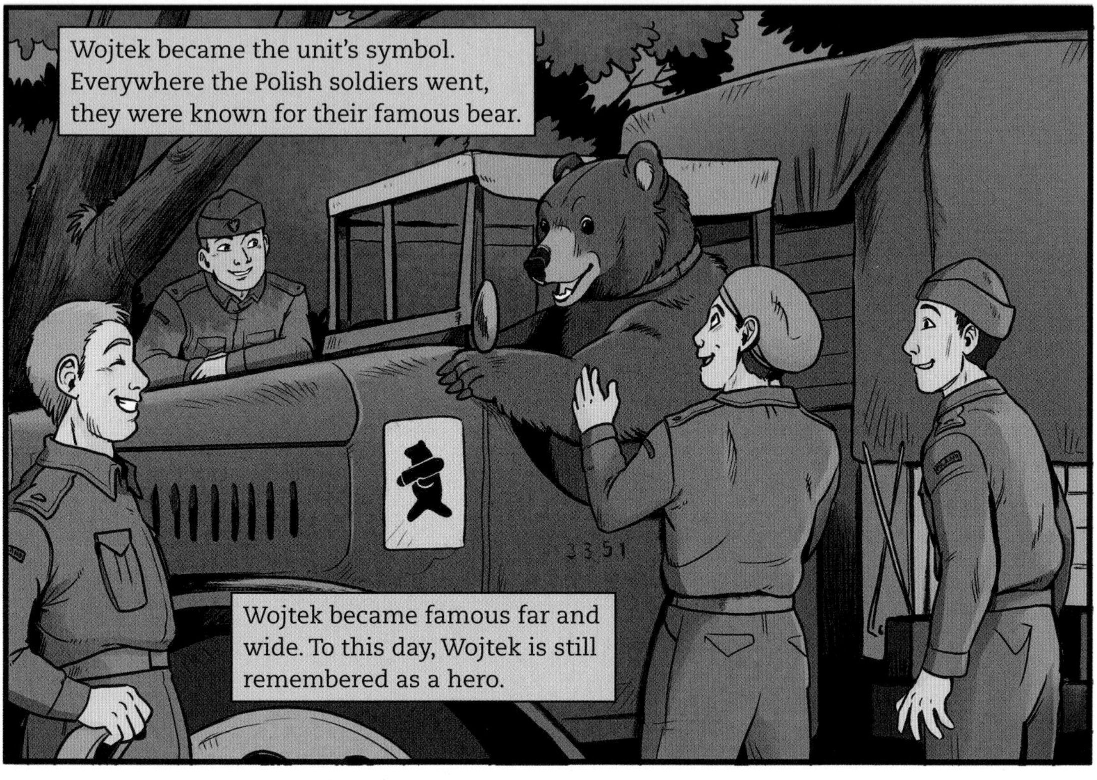
Wojtek became the unit's symbol. Everywhere the Polish soldiers went, they were known for their famous bear.
Wojtek became famous far and wide. To this day, Wojtek is still remembered as a hero.

Chapter 2: A New Friend in a Distant Land

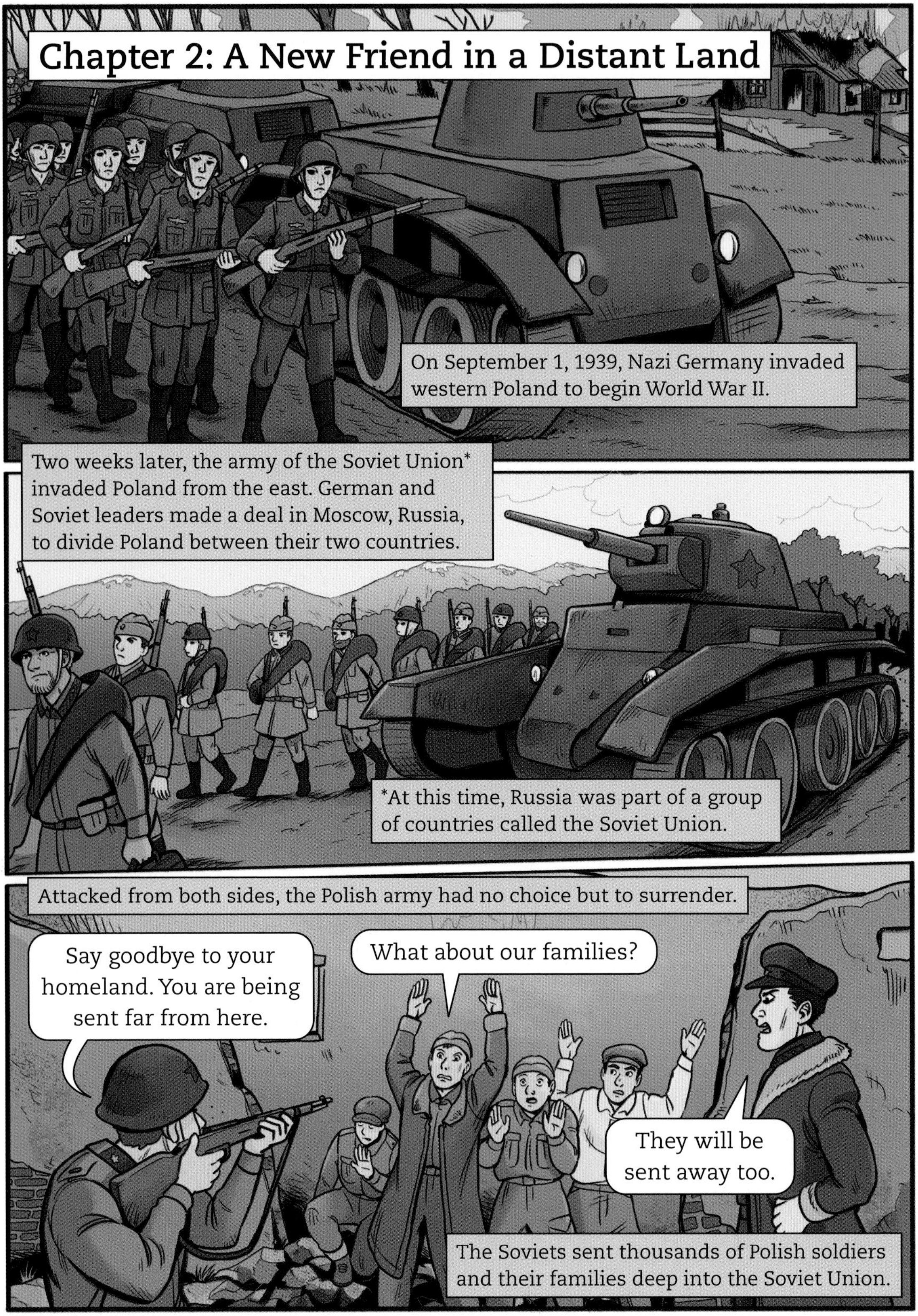

On September 1, 1939, Nazi Germany invaded western Poland to begin World War II.
Two weeks later, the army of the Soviet Union* invaded Poland from the east. German and Soviet leaders made a deal in Moscow, Russia, to divide Poland between their two countries.
*At this time, Russia was part of a group of countries called the Soviet Union.
Attacked from both sides, the Polish army had no choice but to surrender.
Say goodbye to your homeland. You are being sent far from here.
What about our families?
They will be sent away too.
The Soviets sent thousands of Polish soldiers and their families deep into the Soviet Union.

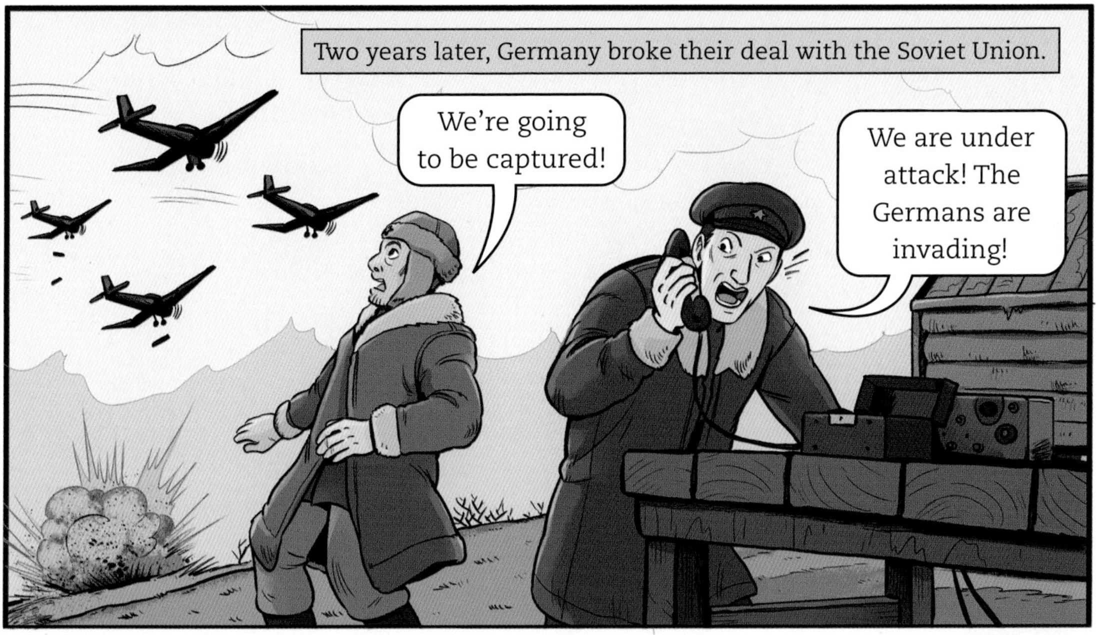
Two years later, Germany broke their deal with the Soviet Union.
We're going to be captured!
We are under attack! The Germans are invading!

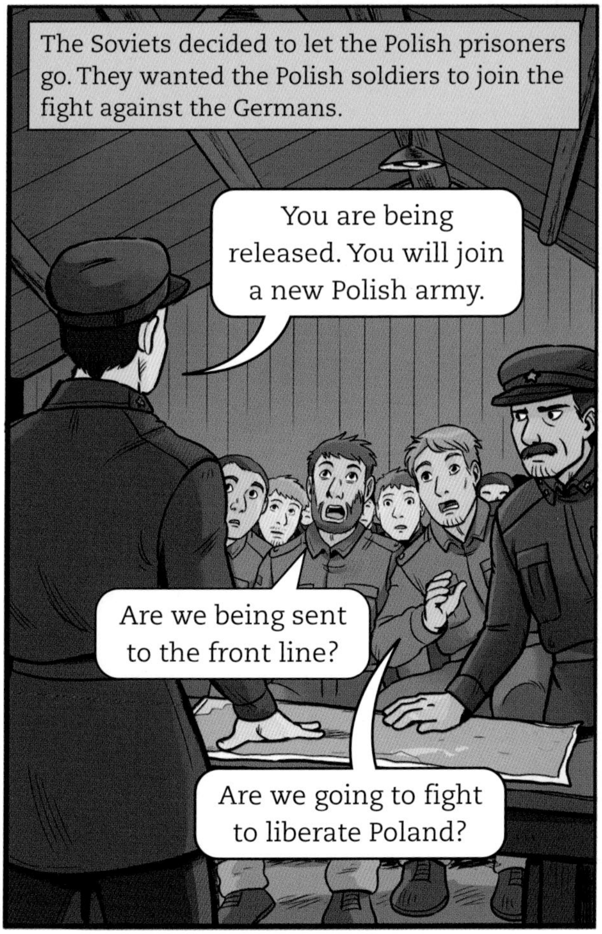
The Soviets decided to let the Polish prisoners go. They wanted the Polish soldiers to join the fight against the Germans.
You are being released. You will join a new Polish army.
Are we being sent to the front line?
Are we going to fight to liberate Poland?

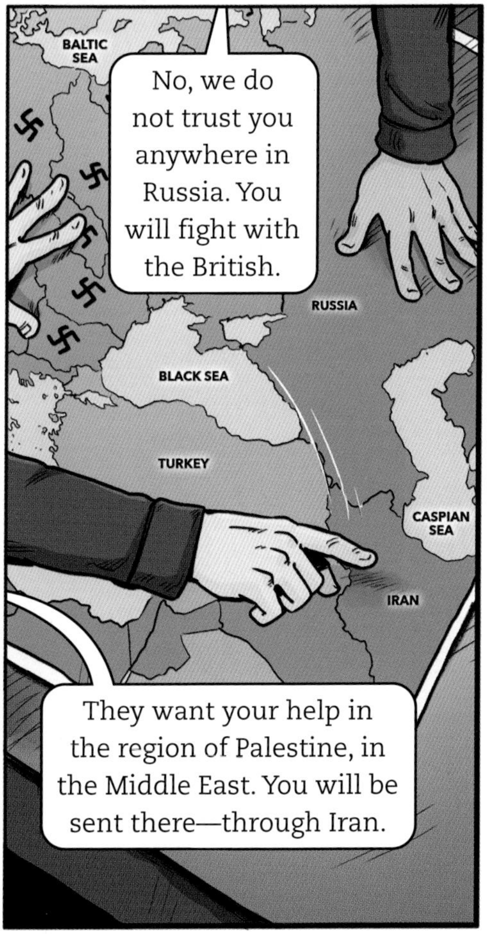
BALTIC SEA
No, we do not trust you anywhere in Russia. You will fight with the British.
RUSSIA
BLACK SEA
TURKEY
CASPIAN SEA
IRAN
They want your help in the region of Palestine, in the Middle East. You will be sent there—through Iran.

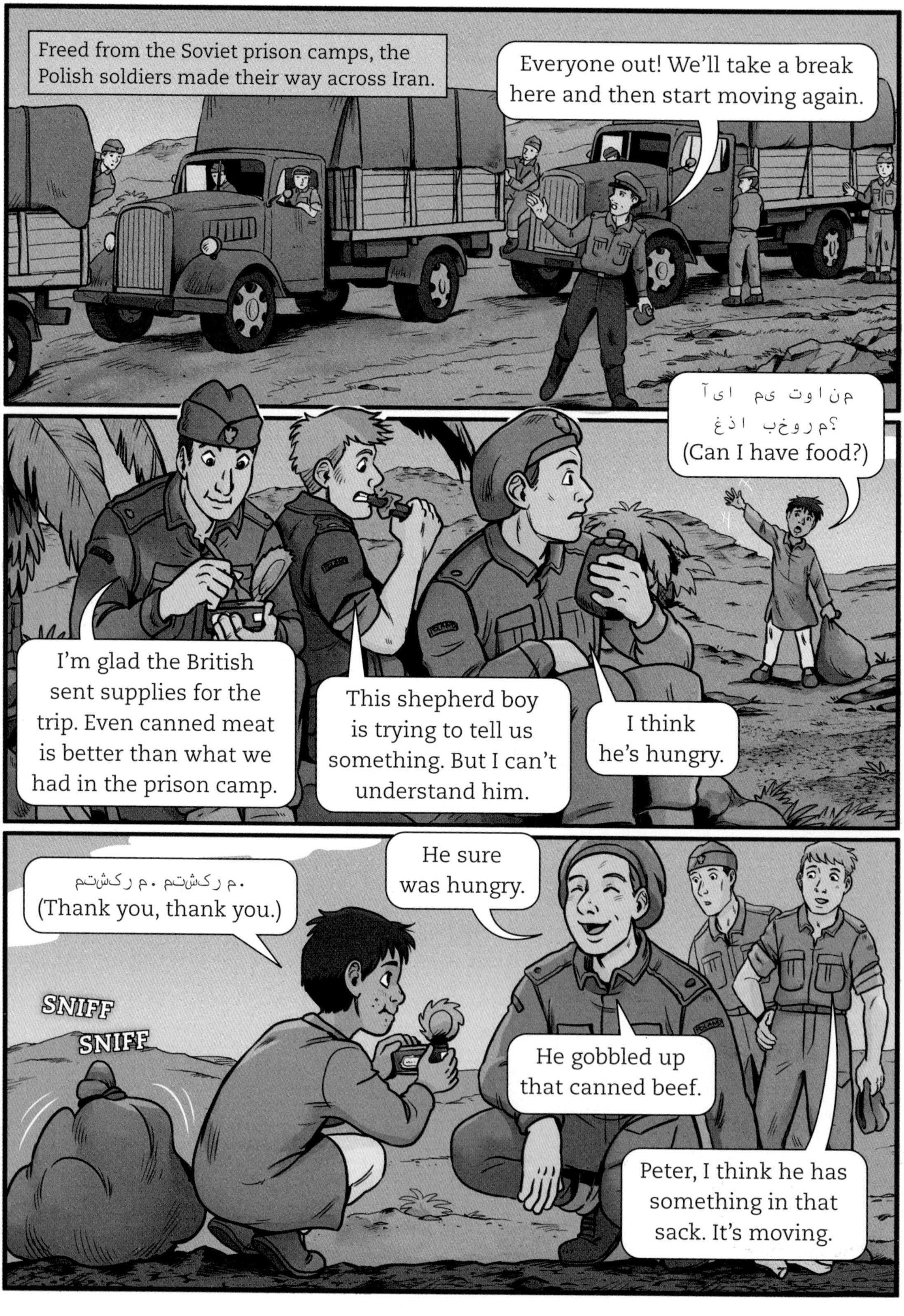

Freed from the Soviet prison camps, the Polish soldiers made their way across Iran.
Everyone out! We'll take a break here and then start moving again.
I'm glad the British sent supplies for the trip. Even canned meat is better than what we had in the prison camp.
This shepherd boy is trying to tell us something. But I can't understand him.
I think he's hungry.
مناوتی م ای آ
مروخب اذغ؟
(Can I have food?)
م رکشتم . م رکشتم.
(Thank you, thank you.)
He sure was hungry.
SNIFF
SNIFF
He gobbled up that canned beef.
Peter, I think he has something in that sack. It's moving.

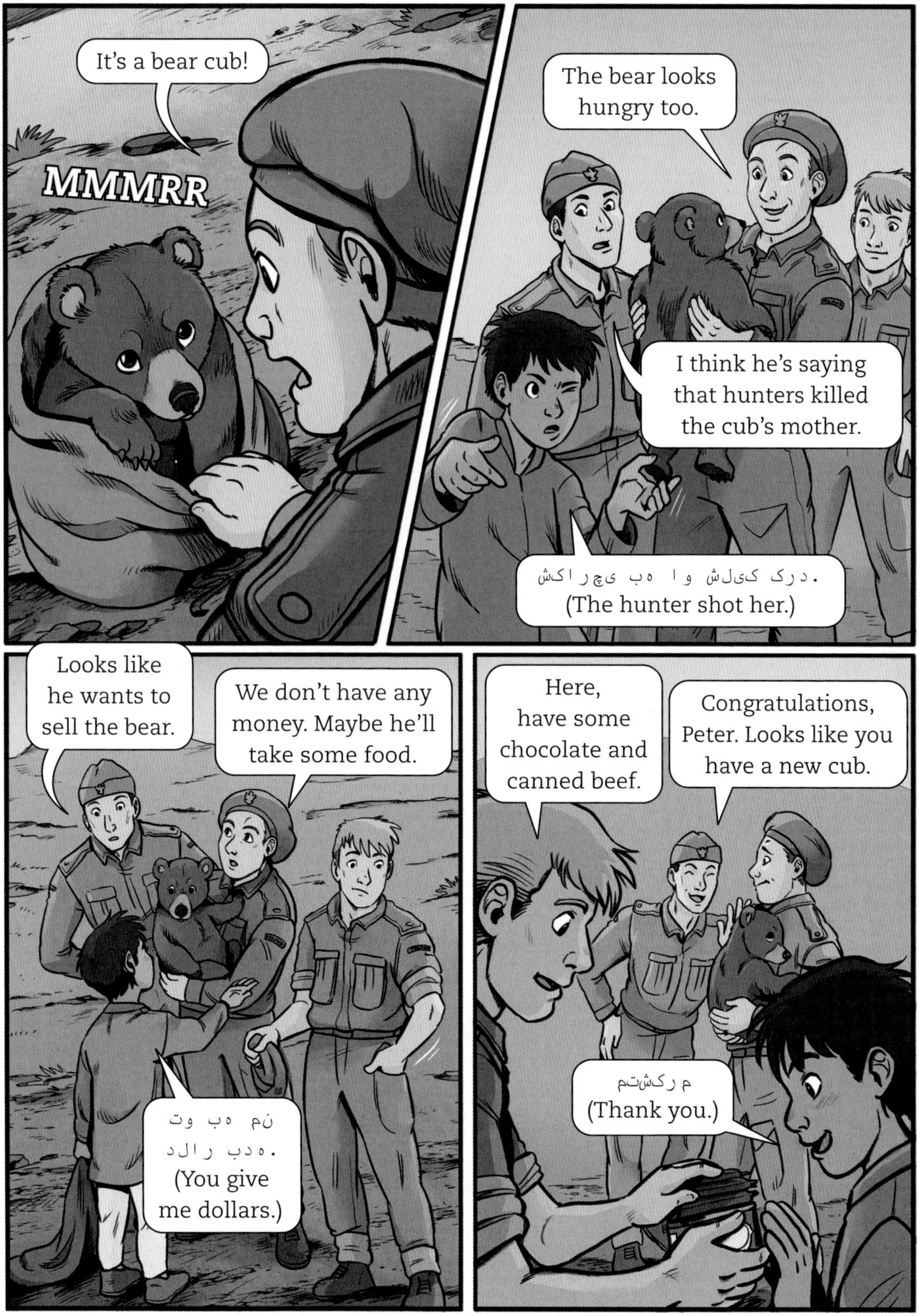
It's a bear cub!
MMMRR
The bear looks hungry too.
I think he's saying that hunters killed the cub's mother.
درک کیلش وا هب یچراکش.
(The hunter shot her.)
Looks like he wants to sell the bear.
We don't have any money. Maybe he'll take some food.
نم هب وت
هدب رالد.
(You give me dollars.)
Here, have some chocolate and canned beef.
Congratulations, Peter. Looks like you have a new cub.
مرکشتم
(Thank you.)

Chapter 3: Tracks Across the Desert

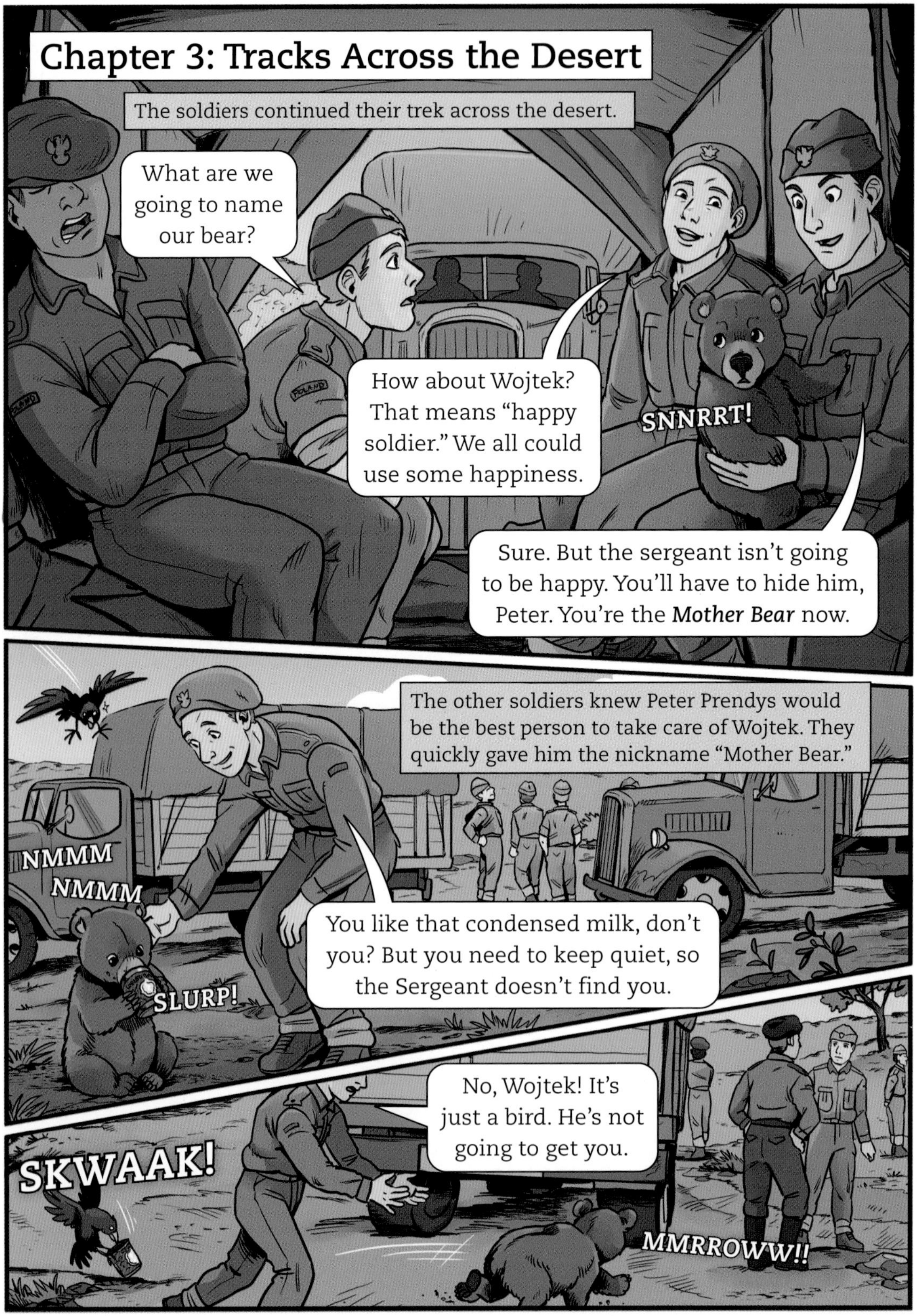
The soldiers continued their trek across the desert.
What are we going to name our bear?
How about Wojtek? That means "happy soldier." We all could use some happiness.
SNNRRT!
Sure. But the sergeant isn't going to be happy. You'll have to hide him, Peter. You're the *Mother Bear* now.
The other soldiers knew Peter Prendys would be the best person to take care of Wojtek. They quickly gave him the nickname "Mother Bear."
NMMM NMMM
You like that condensed milk, don't you? But you need to keep quiet, so the Sergeant doesn't find you.
SLURP!
No, Wojtek! It's just a bird. He's not going to get you.
SKWAAK!
MMRROWW!!

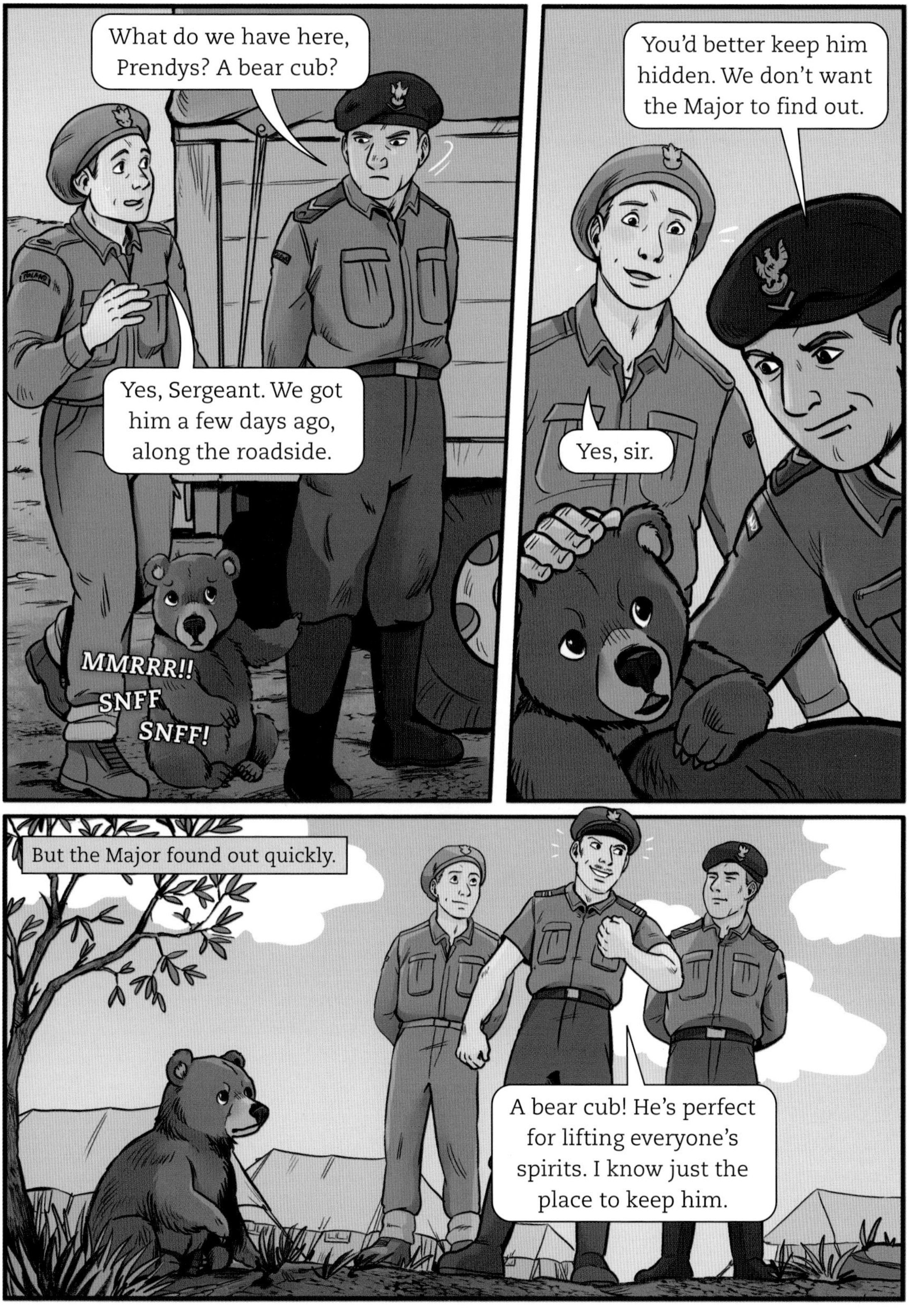
What do we have here, Prendys? A bear cub?
Yes, Sergeant. We got him a few days ago, along the roadside.
MMRRR!!
SNFF
SNFF!
You'd better keep him hidden. We don't want the Major to find out.
Yes, sir.
But the Major found out quickly.
A bear cub! He's perfect for lifting everyone's spirits. I know just the place to keep him.

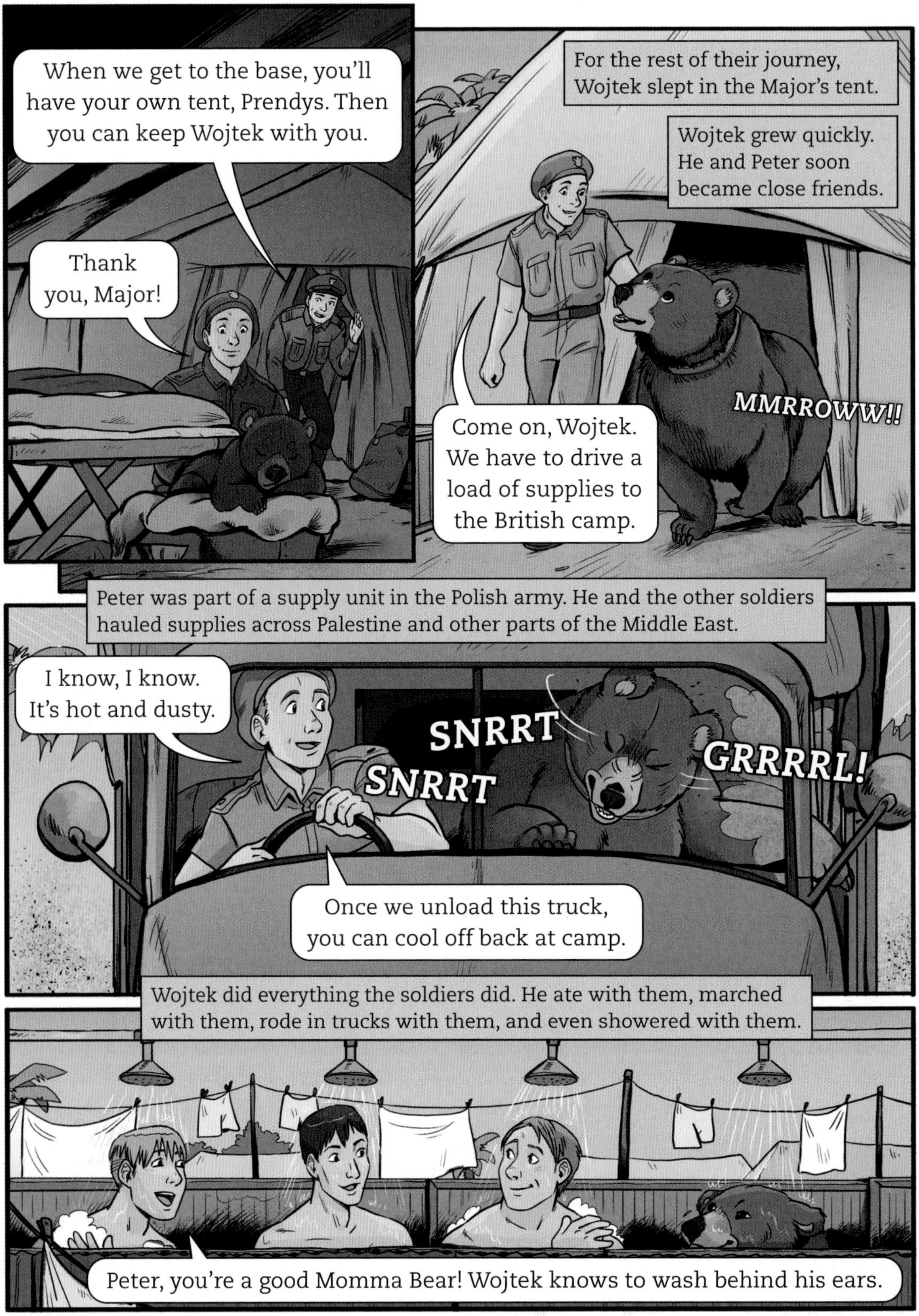
When we get to the base, you'll have your own tent, Prendys. Then you can keep Wojtek with you.
Thank you, Major!
For the rest of their journey, Wojtek slept in the Major's tent.
Wojtek grew quickly. He and Peter soon became close friends.
Come on, Wojtek. We have to drive a load of supplies to the British camp.
MMRROWW!!
Peter was part of a supply unit in the Polish army. He and the other soldiers hauled supplies across Palestine and other parts of the Middle East.
I know, I know. It's hot and dusty.
SNRRT
SNRRT
GRRRRL!
Once we unload this truck, you can cool off back at camp.
Wojtek did everything the soldiers did. He ate with them, marched with them, rode in trucks with them, and even showered with them.
Peter, you're a good Momma Bear! Wojtek knows to wash behind his ears.

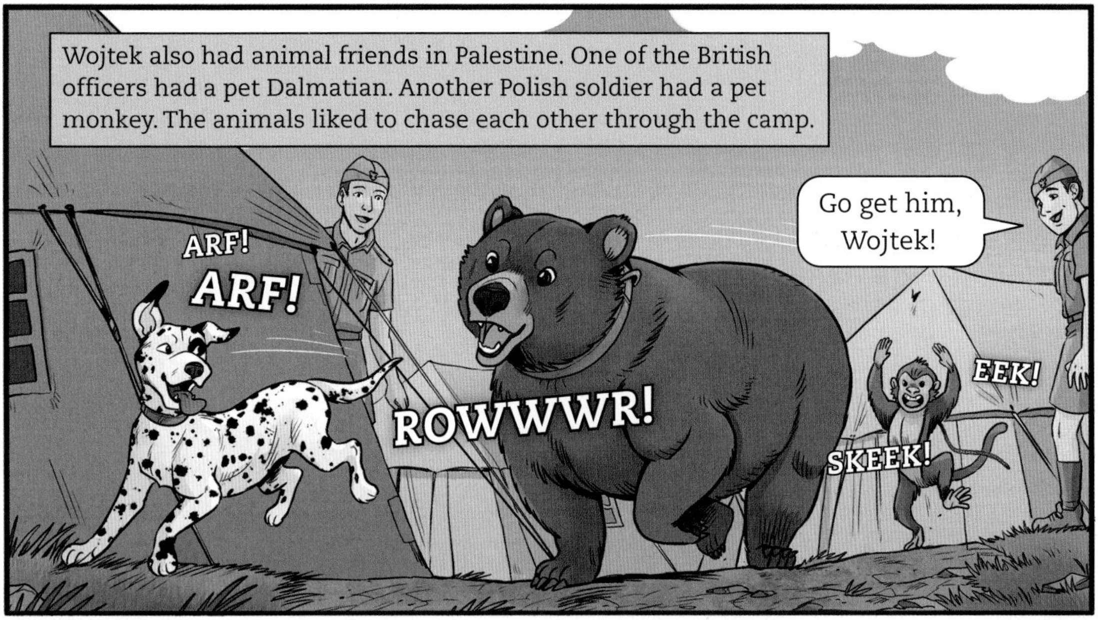
Wojtek also had animal friends in Palestine. One of the British officers had a pet Dalmatian. Another Polish soldier had a pet monkey. The animals liked to chase each other through the camp.
ARF!
ARF!
ROWWWR!
Go get him, Wojtek!
EEK!
SKEEK!

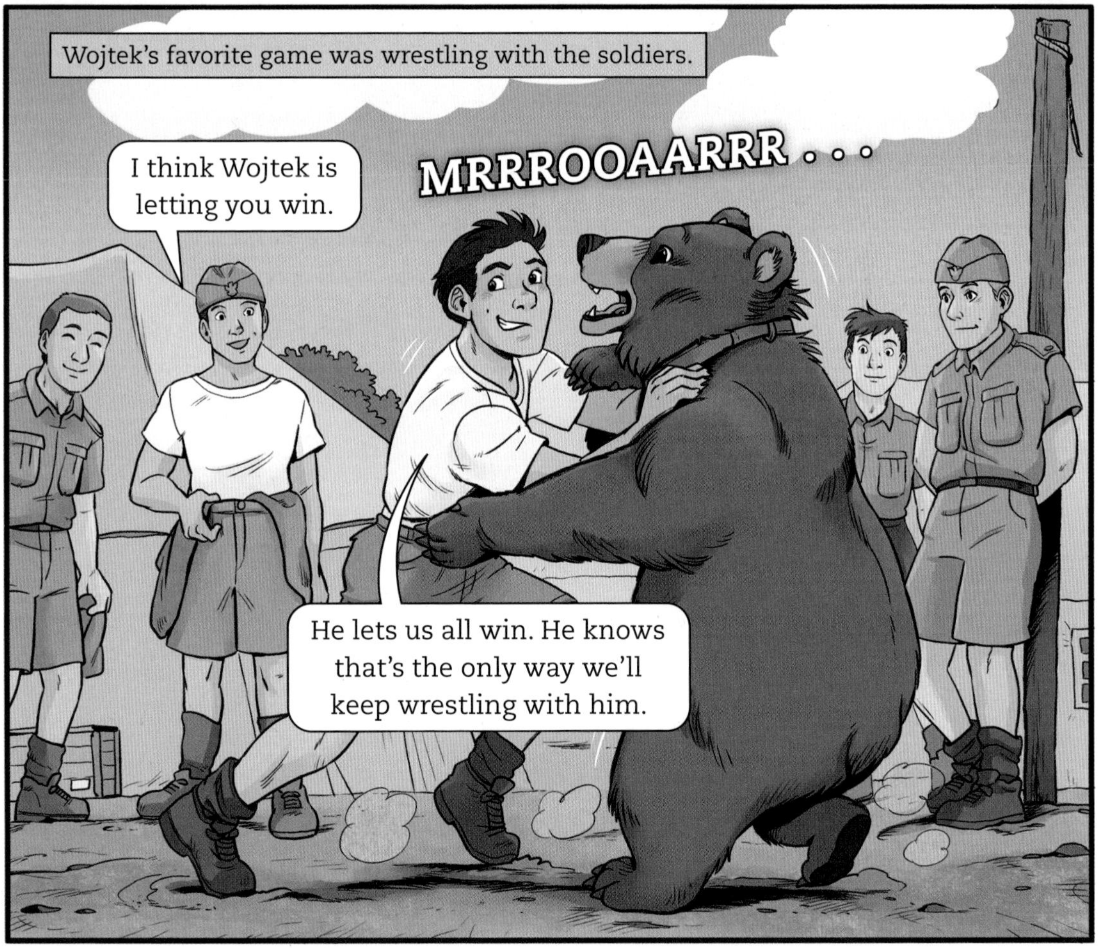
Wojtek's favorite game was wrestling with the soldiers.
I think Wojtek is letting you win.
MRRROOAARRR . . .
He lets us all win. He knows that's the only way we'll keep wrestling with him.

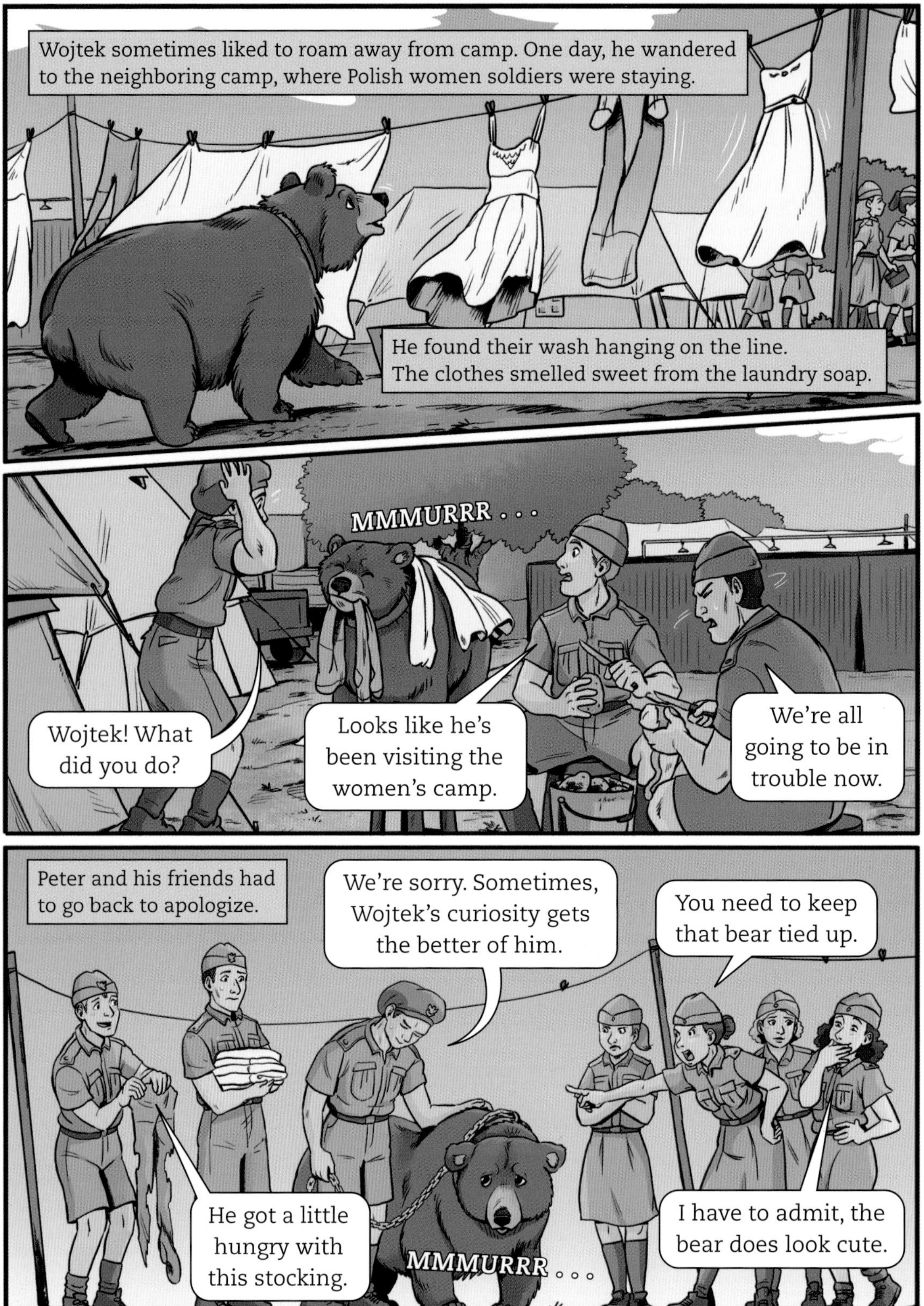
Wojtek sometimes liked to roam away from camp. One day, he wandered to the neighboring camp, where Polish women soldiers were staying.
He found their wash hanging on the line. The clothes smelled sweet from the laundry soap.
MMMURRR . . .
Wojtek! What did you do?
Looks like he's been visiting the women's camp.
We're all going to be in trouble now.
Peter and his friends had to go back to apologize.
We're sorry. Sometimes, Wojtek's curiosity gets the better of him.
You need to keep that bear tied up.
He got a little hungry with this stocking.
MMMURRR . . .
I have to admit, the bear does look cute.

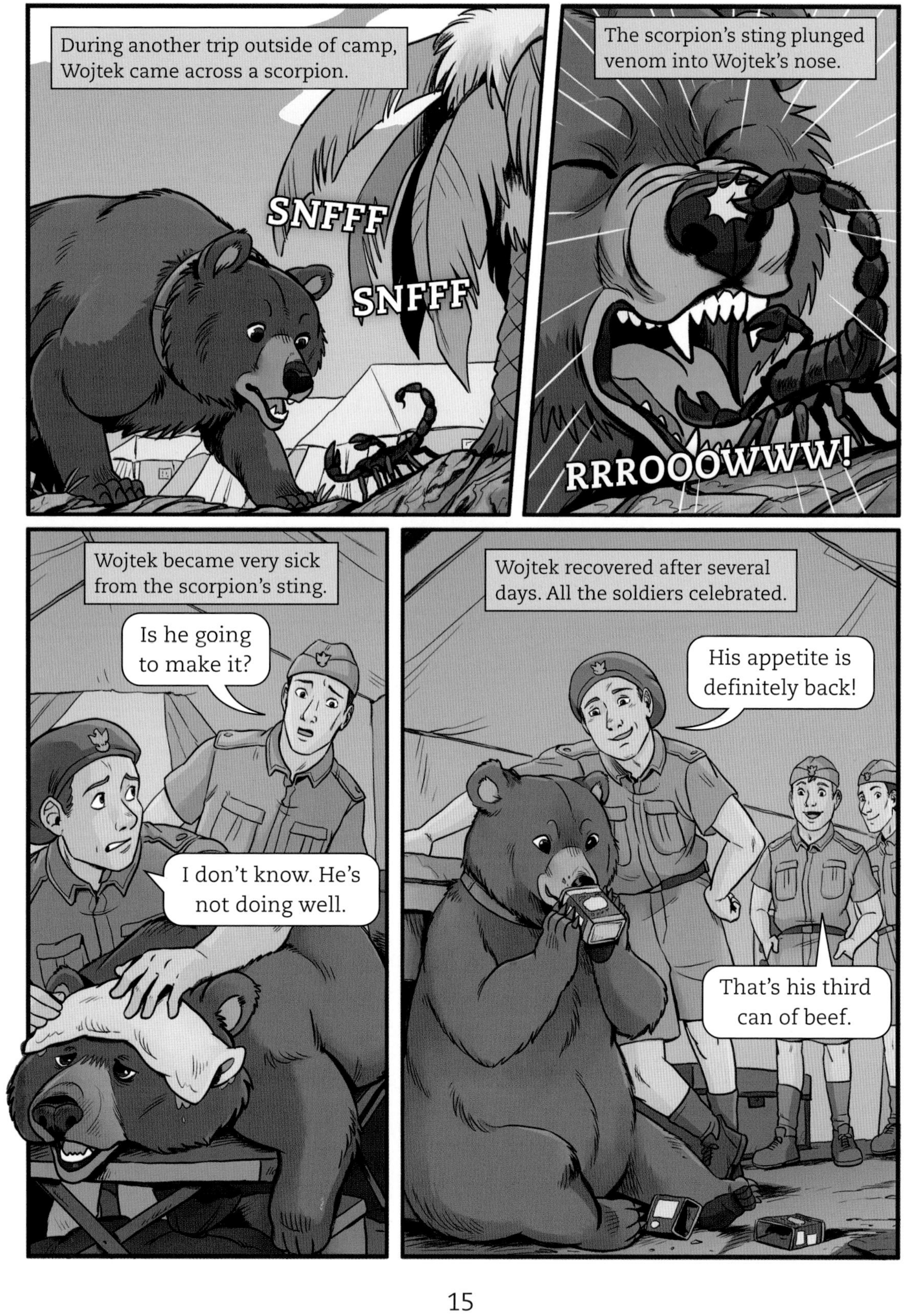
During another trip outside of camp, Wojtek came across a scorpion.
SNFFF
SNFFF
The scorpion's sting plunged venom into Wojtek's nose.
RRROOOWWW!
Wojtek became very sick from the scorpion's sting.
Is he going to make it?
I don't know. He's not doing well.
Wojtek recovered after several days. All the soldiers celebrated.
His appetite is definitely back!
That's his third can of beef.

Chapter 4: Wojtek Joins the Army

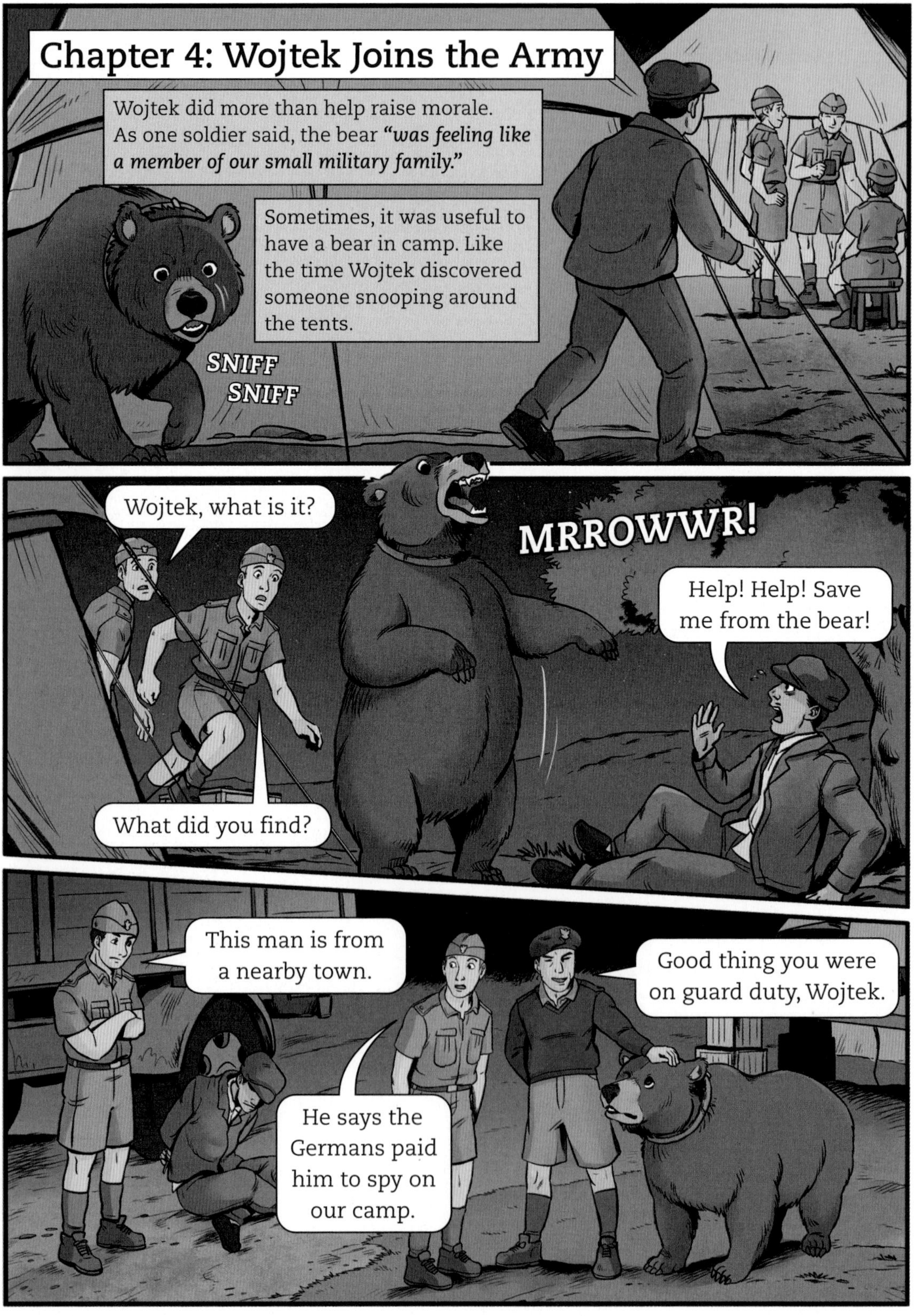
Wojtek did more than help raise morale. As one soldier said, the bear ***"was feeling like a member of our small military family."***
Sometimes, it was useful to have a bear in camp. Like the time Wojtek discovered someone snooping around the tents.
SNIFF SNIFF
Wojtek, what is it?
MRROWWR!
Help! Help! Save me from the bear!
What did you find?
This man is from a nearby town.
Good thing you were on guard duty, Wojtek.
He says the Germans paid him to spy on our camp.

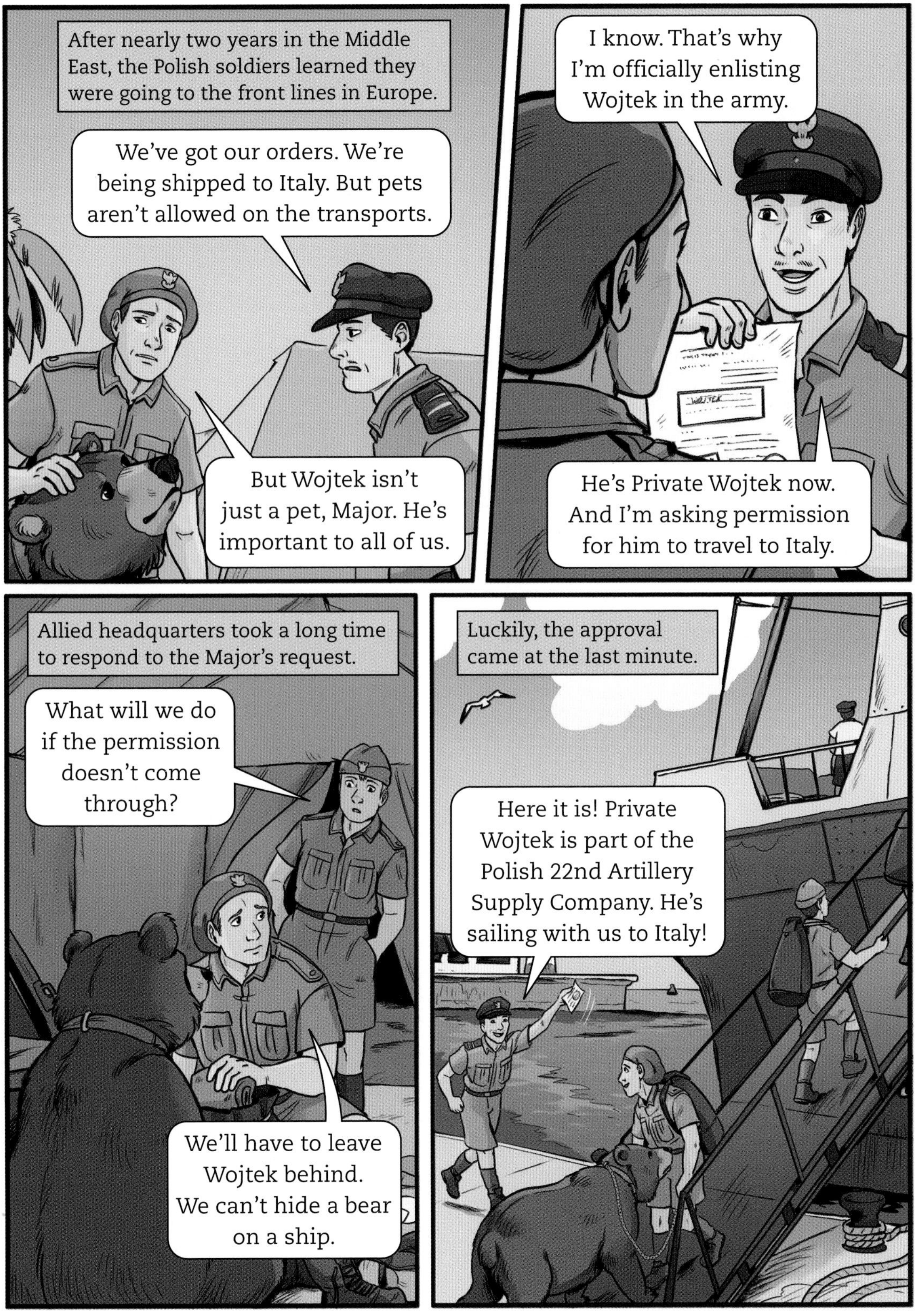
After nearly two years in the Middle East, the Polish soldiers learned they were going to the front lines in Europe.
We've got our orders. We're being shipped to Italy. But pets aren't allowed on the transports.
But Wojtek isn't just a pet, Major. He's important to all of us.
I know. That's why I'm officially enlisting Wojtek in the army.
He's Private Wojtek now. And I'm asking permission for him to travel to Italy.
Allied headquarters took a long time to respond to the Major's request.
What will we do if the permission doesn't come through?
We'll have to leave Wojtek behind. We can't hide a bear on a ship.
Luckily, the approval came at the last minute.
Here it is! Private Wojtek is part of the Polish 22nd Artillery Supply Company. He's sailing with us to Italy!

Wojtek and the Polish soldiers landed in southern Italy in 1944.

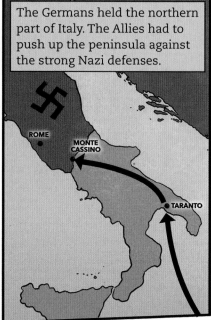

The Germans held the northern part of Italy. The Allies had to push up the peninsula against the strong Nazi defenses.

ROME

MONTE CASSINO

TARANTO

The Allied army had soldiers from many different countries including Canada, Brazil, India, Morocco, New Zealand, Britain, and the United States.

Like always, Wojtek explored the camp in search of something to eat or someone to play with.

Wojtek, where are you?

But not everyone realized the bear was friendly.

A bear!

Don't shoot!

That's our bear!

MRROWWR?

What is a bear doing here?

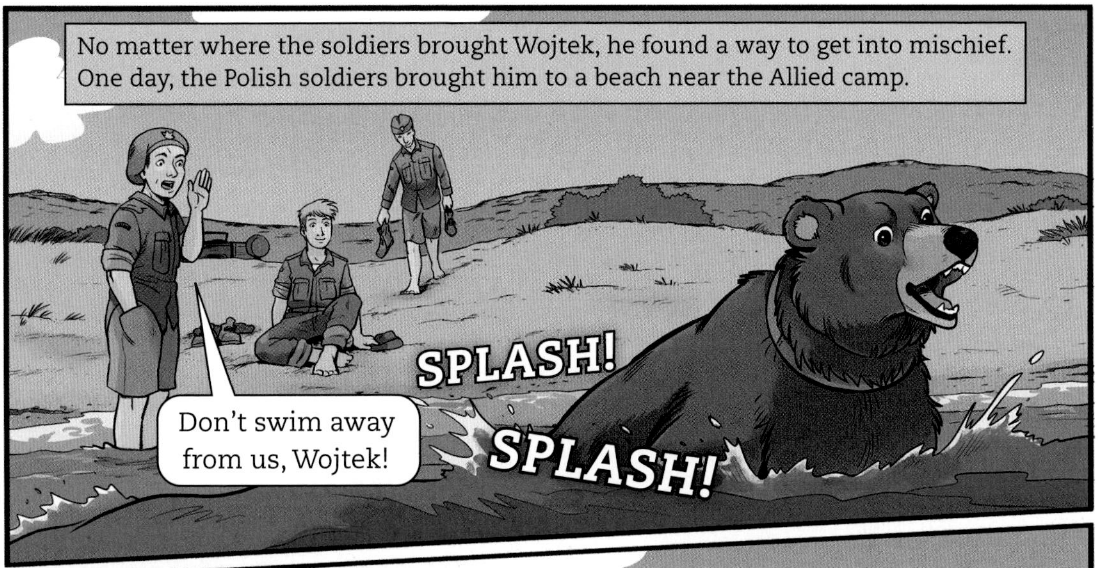
No matter where the soldiers brought Wojtek, he found a way to get into mischief. One day, the Polish soldiers brought him to a beach near the Allied camp.
SPLASH!
Don't swim away from us, Wojtek!
SPLASH!

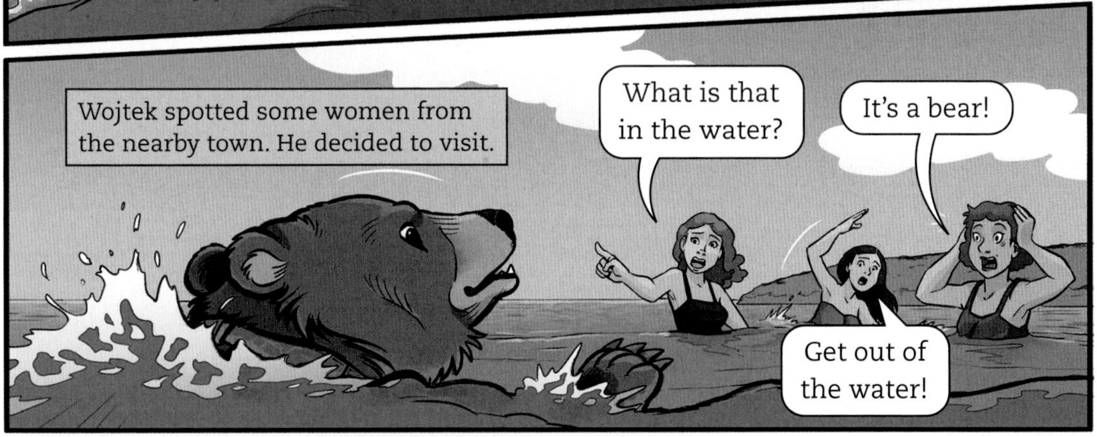
Wojtek spotted some women from the nearby town. He decided to visit.
What is that in the water?
It's a bear!
Get out of the water!

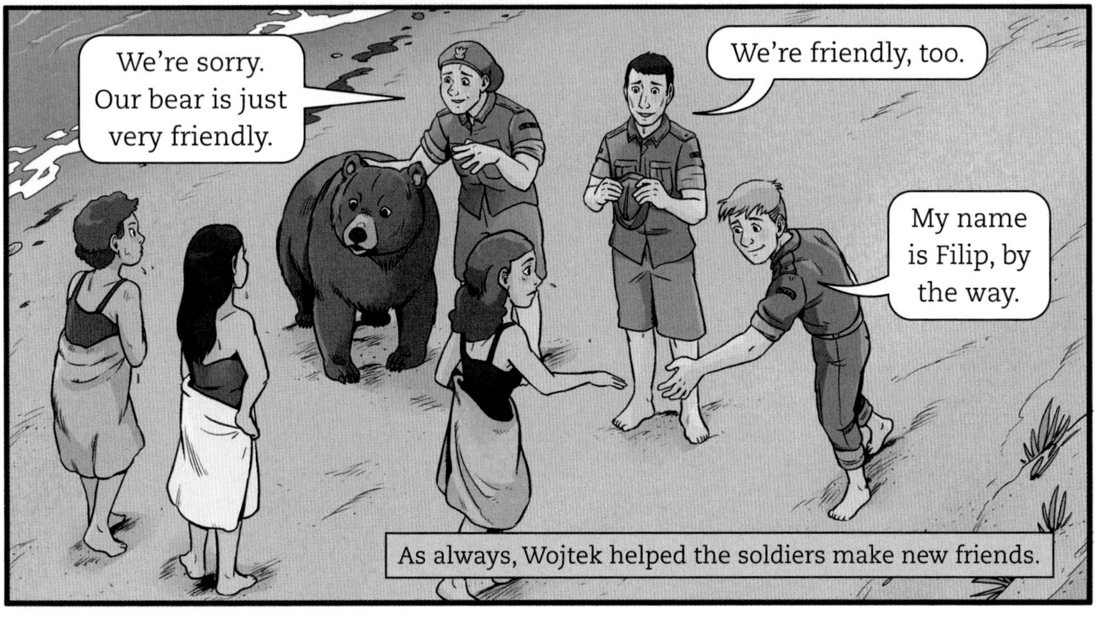
We're sorry. Our bear is just very friendly.
We're friendly, too.
My name is Filip, by the way.
As always, Wojtek helped the soldiers make new friends.

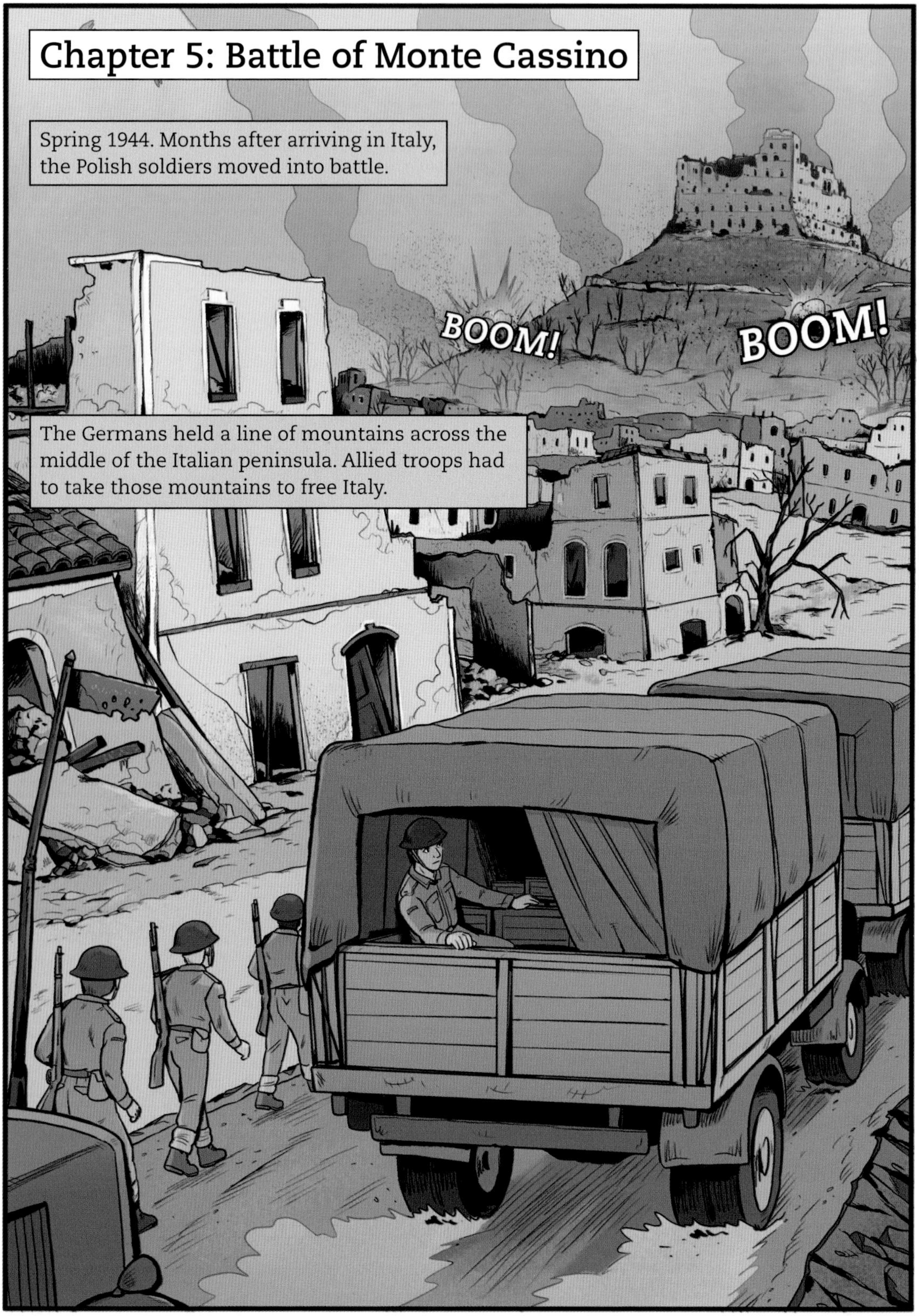
Chapter 5: Battle of Monte Cassino
Spring 1944. Months after arriving in Italy, the Polish soldiers moved into battle.
BOOM!
BOOM!
The Germans held a line of mountains across the middle of the Italian peninsula. Allied troops had to take those mountains to free Italy.

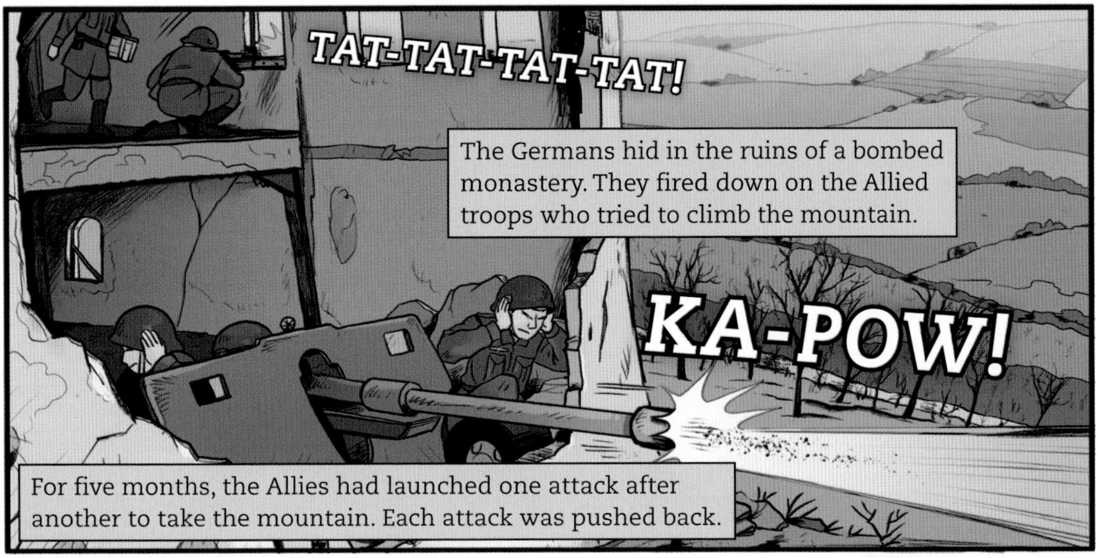
TAT-TAT-TAT-TAT!
The Germans hid in the ruins of a bombed monastery. They fired down on the Allied troops who tried to climb the mountain.
KA-POW!
For five months, the Allies had launched one attack after another to take the mountain. Each attack was pushed back.

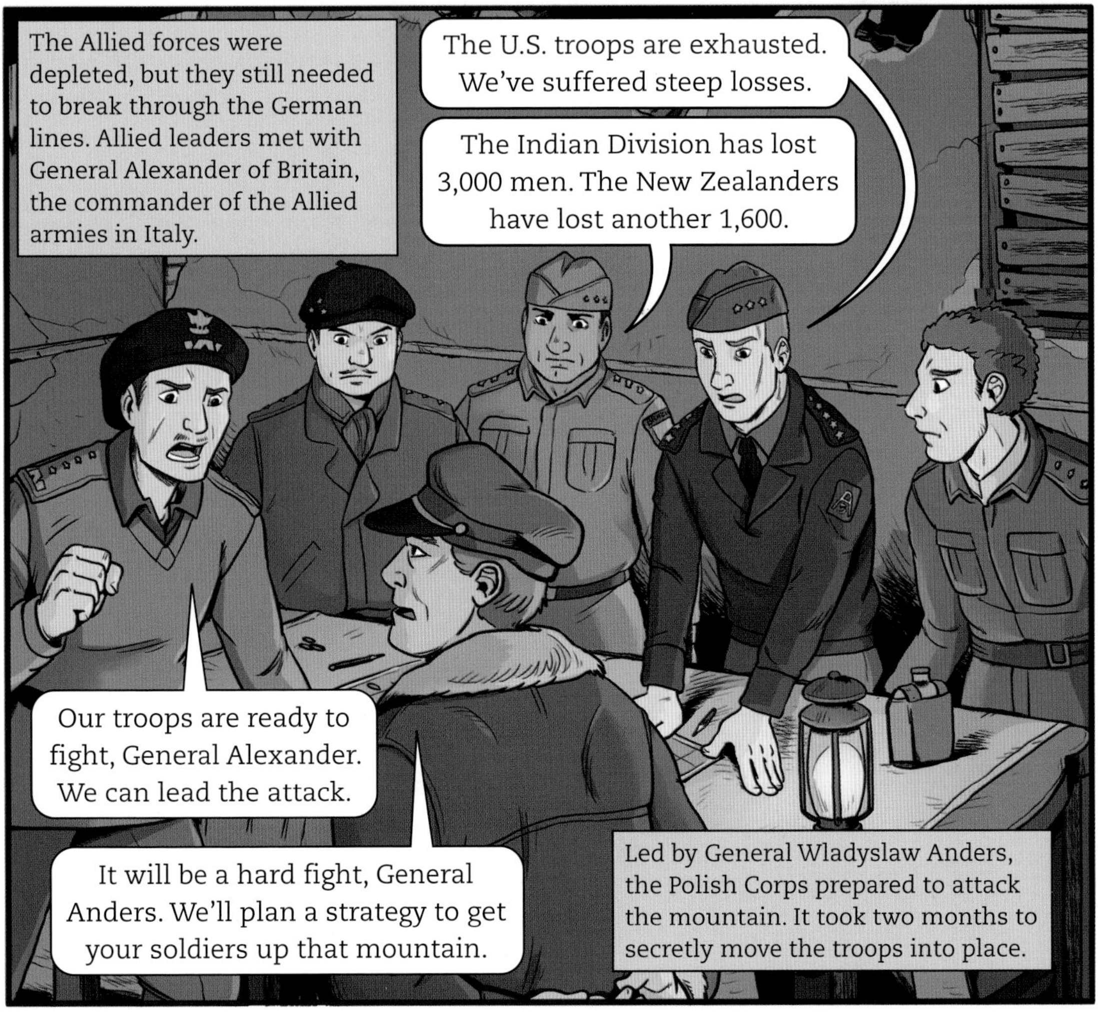
The Allied forces were depleted, but they still needed to break through the German lines. Allied leaders met with General Alexander of Britain, the commander of the Allied armies in Italy.
The U.S. troops are exhausted. We've suffered steep losses.
The Indian Division has lost 3,000 men. The New Zealanders have lost another 1,600.
Our troops are ready to fight, General Alexander. We can lead the attack.
It will be a hard fight, General Anders. We'll plan a strategy to get your soldiers up that mountain.
Led by General Wladyslaw Anders, the Polish Corps prepared to attack the mountain. It took two months to secretly move the troops into place.

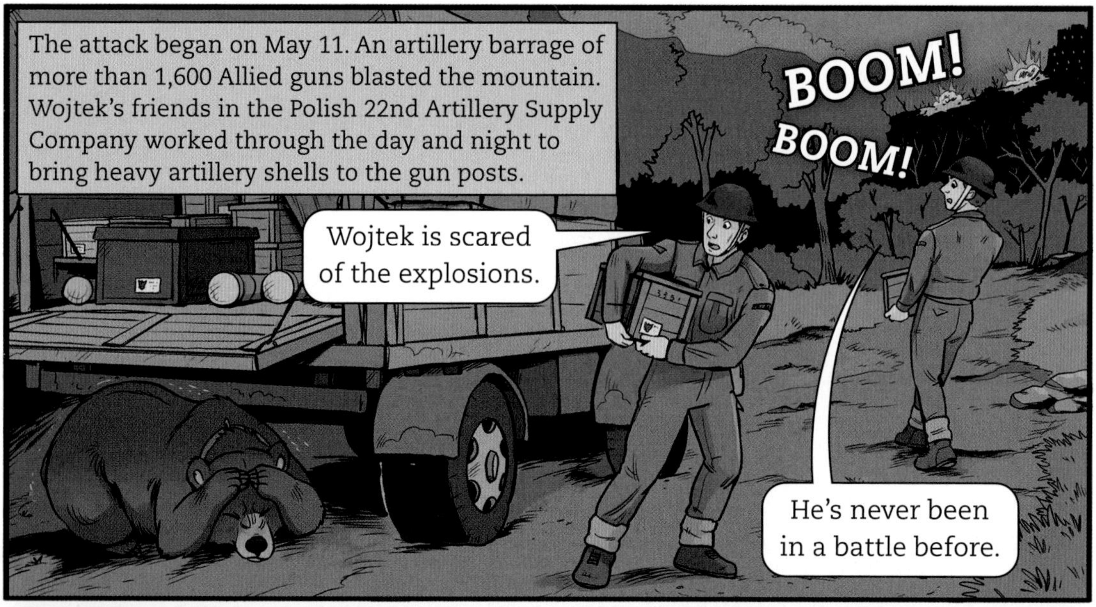
The attack began on May 11. An artillery barrage of more than 1,600 Allied guns blasted the mountain. Wojtek's friends in the Polish 22nd Artillery Supply Company worked through the day and night to bring heavy artillery shells to the gun posts.
BOOM!
BOOM!
Wojtek is scared of the explosions.
He's never been in a battle before.

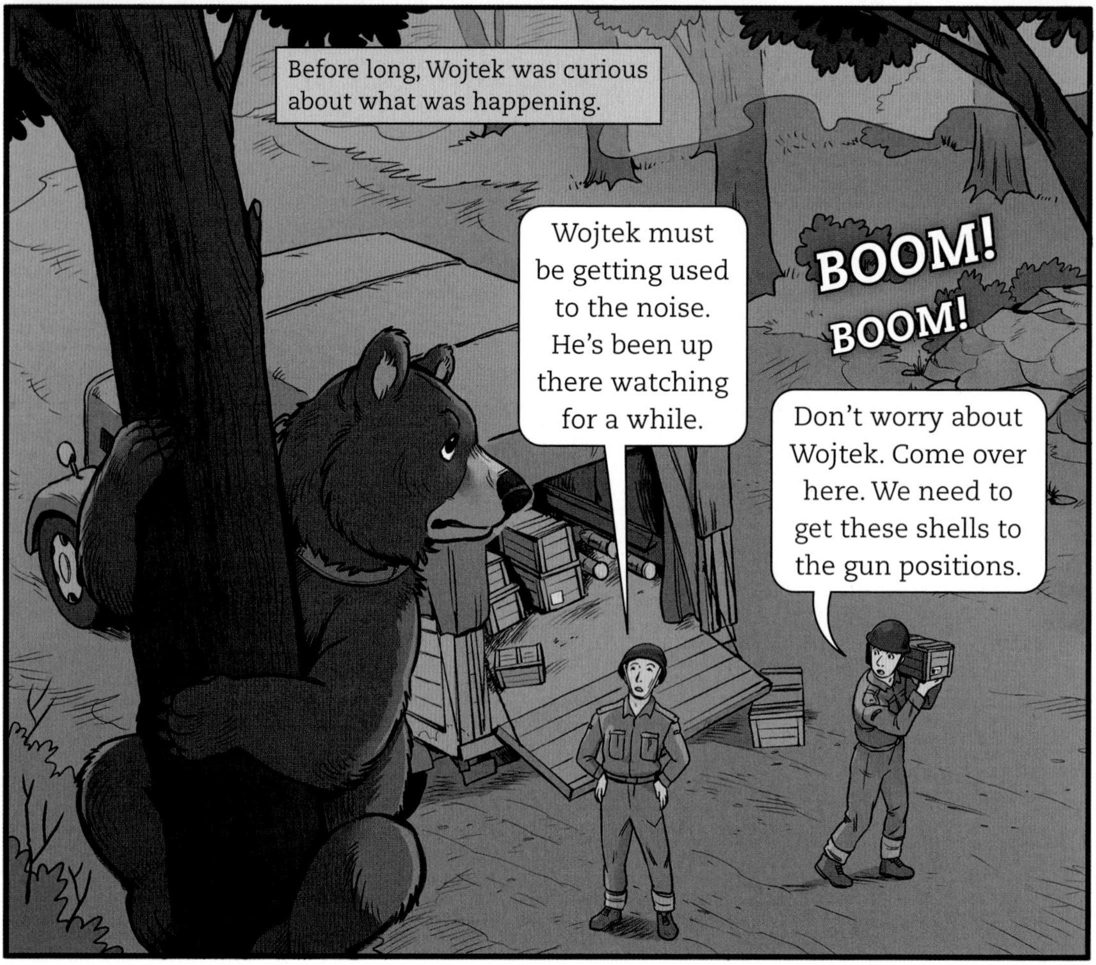
Before long, Wojtek was curious about what was happening.
Wojtek must be getting used to the noise. He's been up there watching for a while.
BOOM!
BOOM!
Don't worry about Wojtek. Come over here. We need to get these shells to the gun positions.

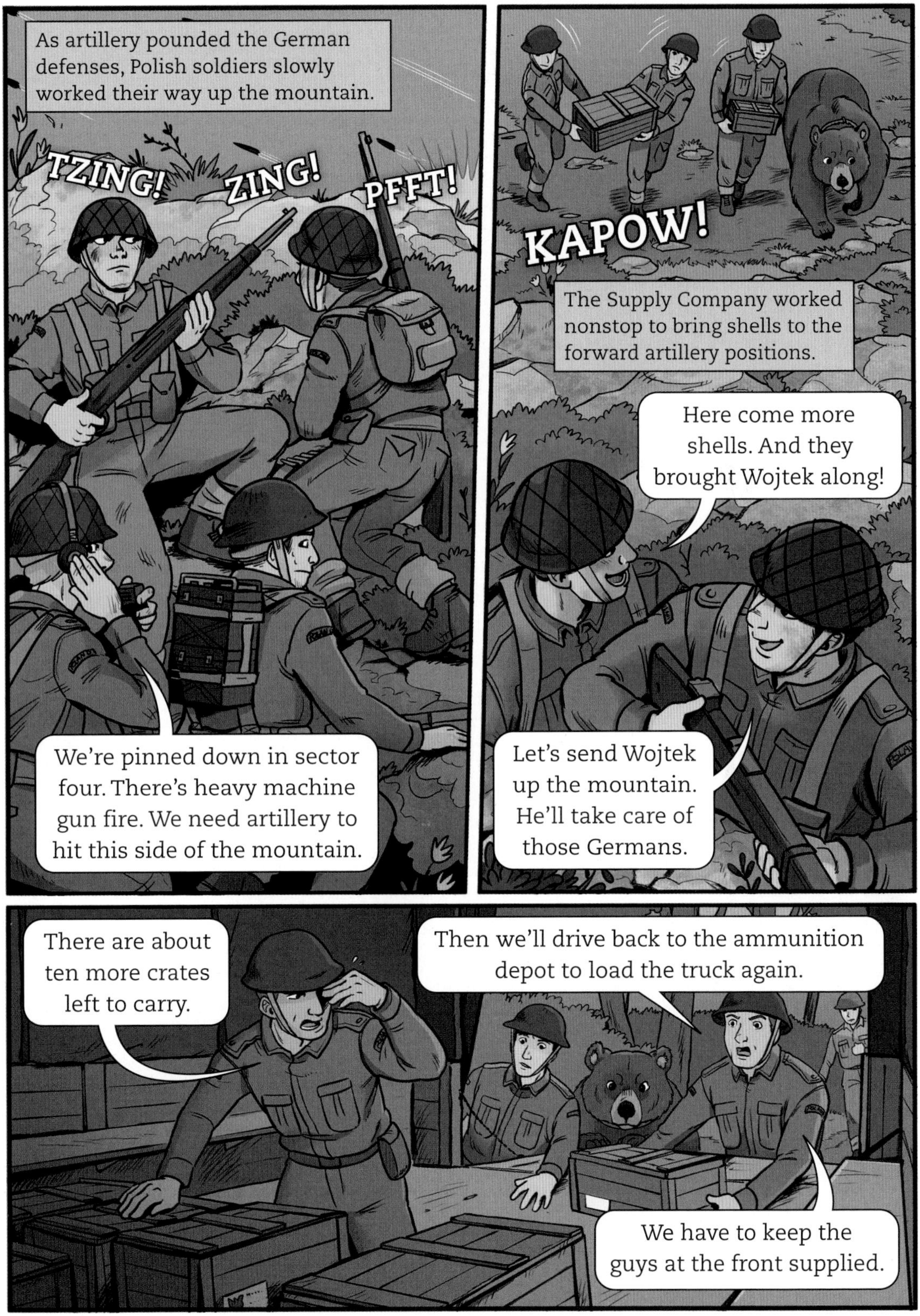
As artillery pounded the German defenses, Polish soldiers slowly worked their way up the mountain.
TZING!
ZING!
PFFT!
We're pinned down in sector four. There's heavy machine gun fire. We need artillery to hit this side of the mountain.
KAPOW!
The Supply Company worked nonstop to bring shells to the forward artillery positions.
Here come more shells. And they brought Wojtek along!
Let's send Wojtek up the mountain. He'll take care of those Germans.
There are about ten more crates left to carry.
Then we'll drive back to the ammunition depot to load the truck again.
We have to keep the guys at the front supplied.

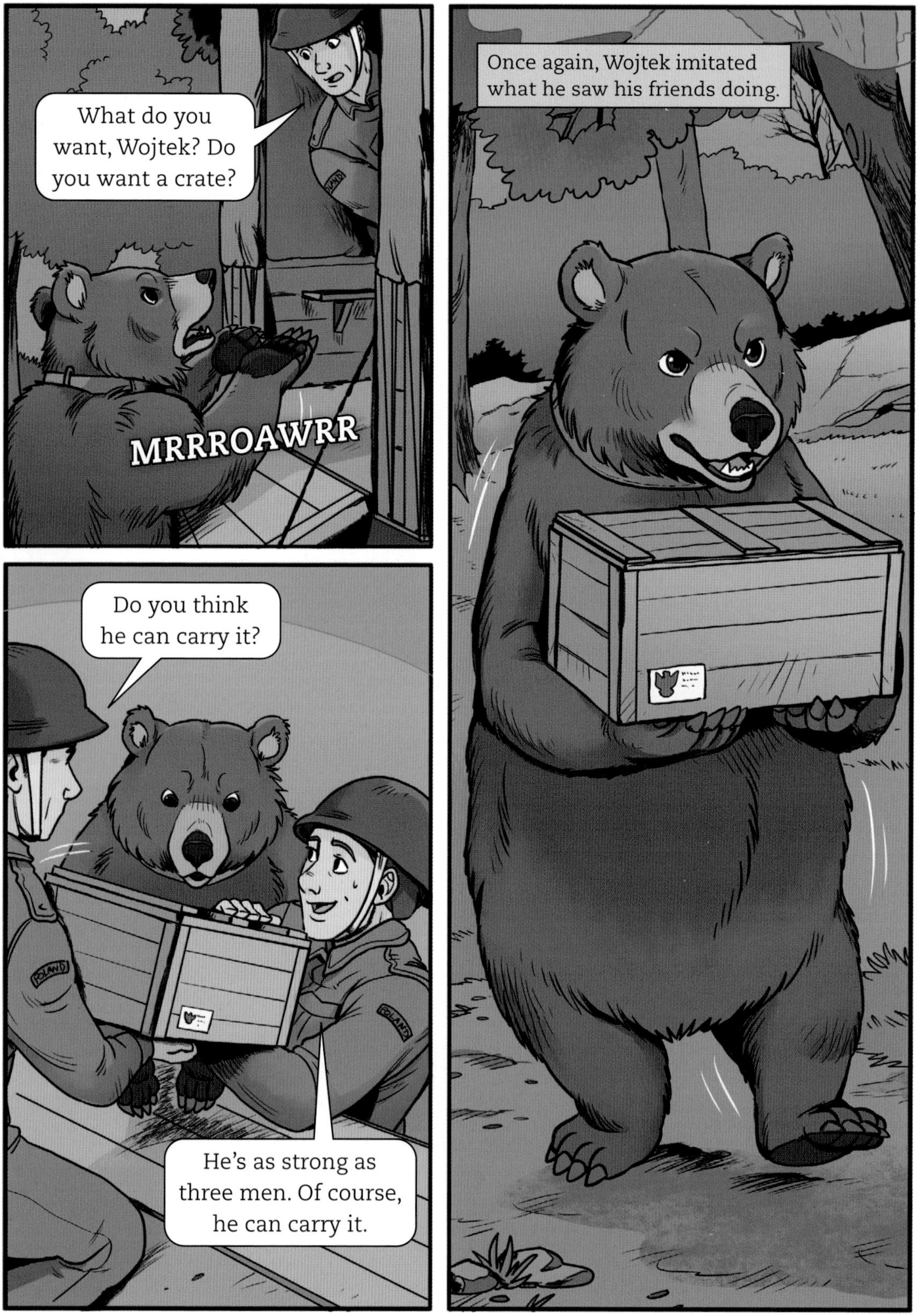
What do you want, Wojtek? Do you want a crate?
MRRROAWRR
Do you think he can carry it?
He's as strong as three men. Of course, he can carry it.
Once again, Wojtek imitated what he saw his friends doing.

During the battle, Wojtek carried crates and single shells. Soldiers from the other Allied armies couldn't believe what they saw.

Is that a bear coming out of the woods? It looks like it's carrying something.

Hey, look out! There's a bear coming!

It's okay! That's our bear!

It's headed for that artillery position over there.

The Allied attack on Monte Cassino lasted a week. Wojtek's supply company brought more than 17,000 tons of ammunition to soldiers on the front lines.

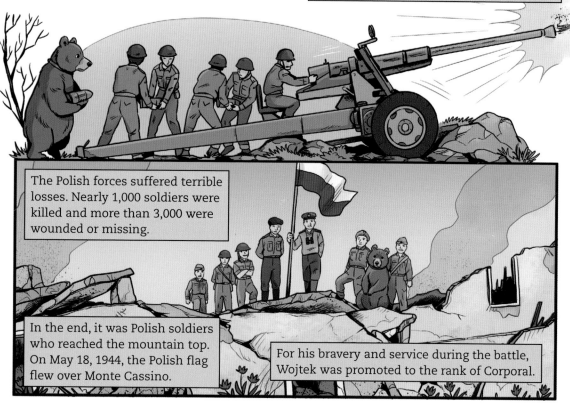

The Polish forces suffered terrible losses. Nearly 1,000 soldiers were killed and more than 3,000 were wounded or missing.

In the end, it was Polish soldiers who reached the mountain top. On May 18, 1944, the Polish flag flew over Monte Cassino.

For his bravery and service during the battle, Wojtek was promoted to the rank of Corporal.

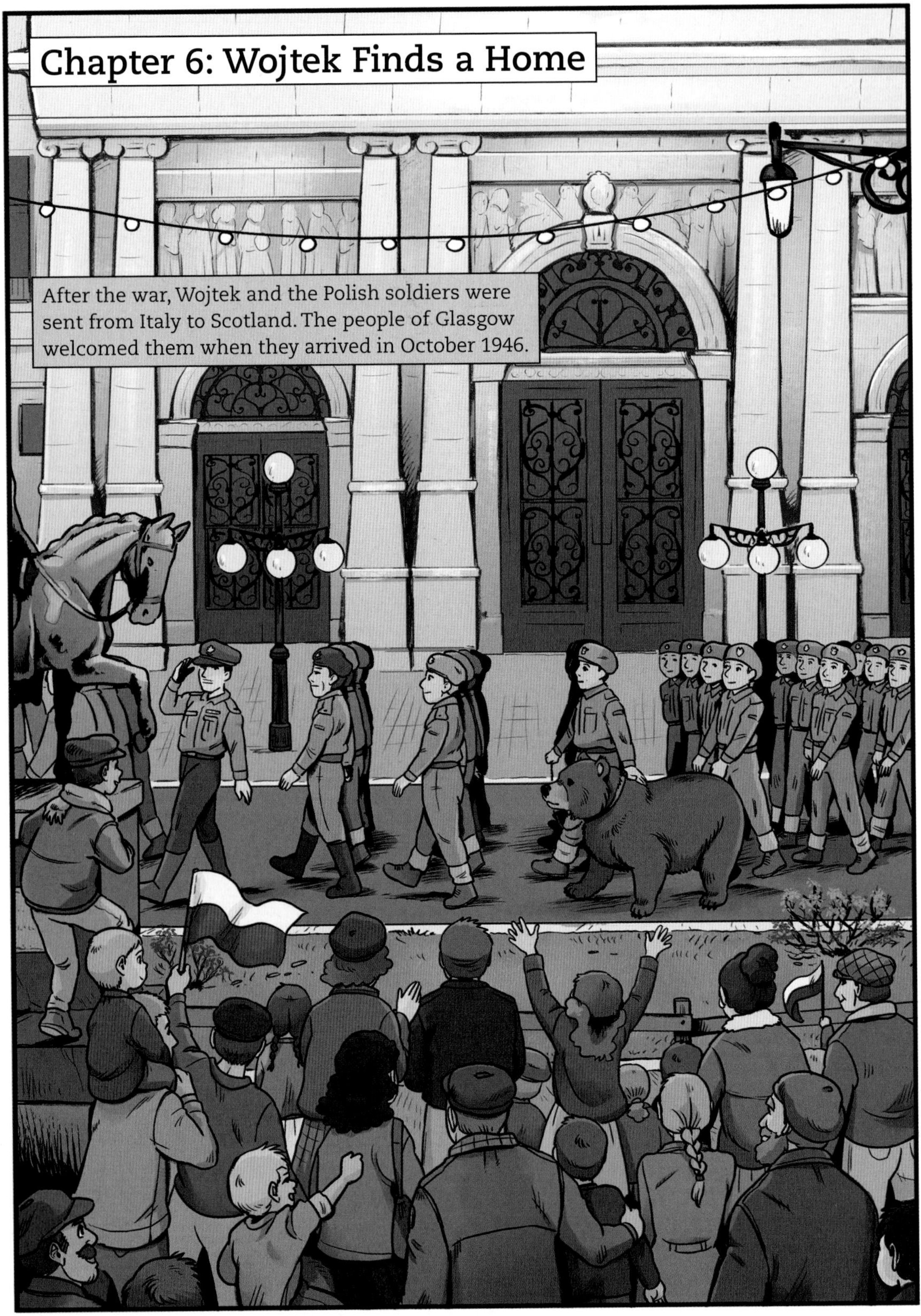
Chapter 6: Wojtek Finds a Home
After the war, Wojtek and the Polish soldiers were sent from Italy to Scotland. The people of Glasgow welcomed them when they arrived in October 1946.

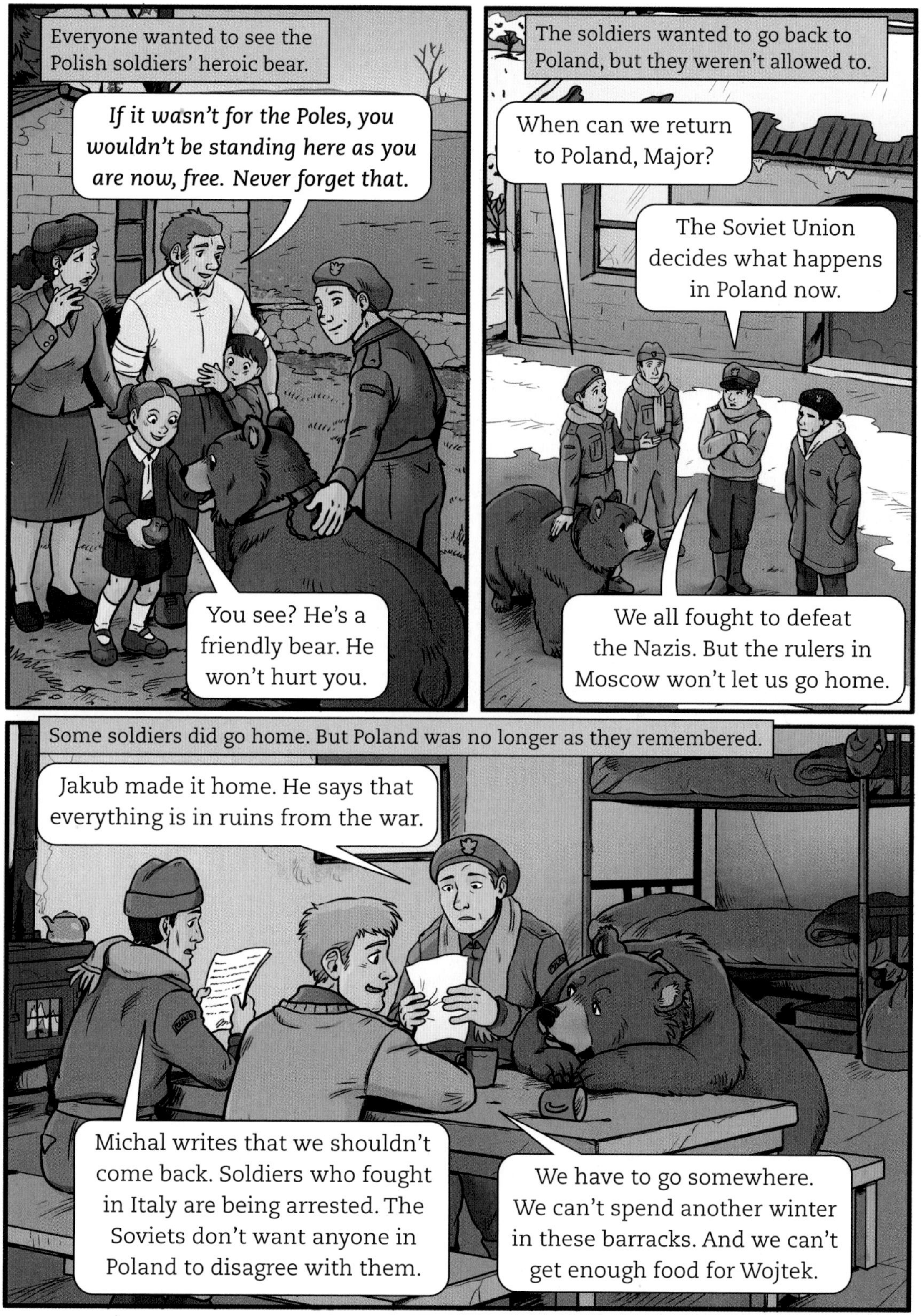
Everyone wanted to see the Polish soldiers' heroic bear.
If it wasn't for the Poles, you wouldn't be standing here as you are now, free. Never forget that.
You see? He's a friendly bear. He won't hurt you.
The soldiers wanted to go back to Poland, but they weren't allowed to.
When can we return to Poland, Major?
The Soviet Union decides what happens in Poland now.
We all fought to defeat the Nazis. But the rulers in Moscow won't let us go home.
Some soldiers did go home. But Poland was no longer as they remembered.
Jakub made it home. He says that everything is in ruins from the war.
Michal writes that we shouldn't come back. Soldiers who fought in Italy are being arrested. The Soviets don't want anyone in Poland to disagree with them.
We have to go somewhere. We can't spend another winter in these barracks. And we can't get enough food for Wojtek.

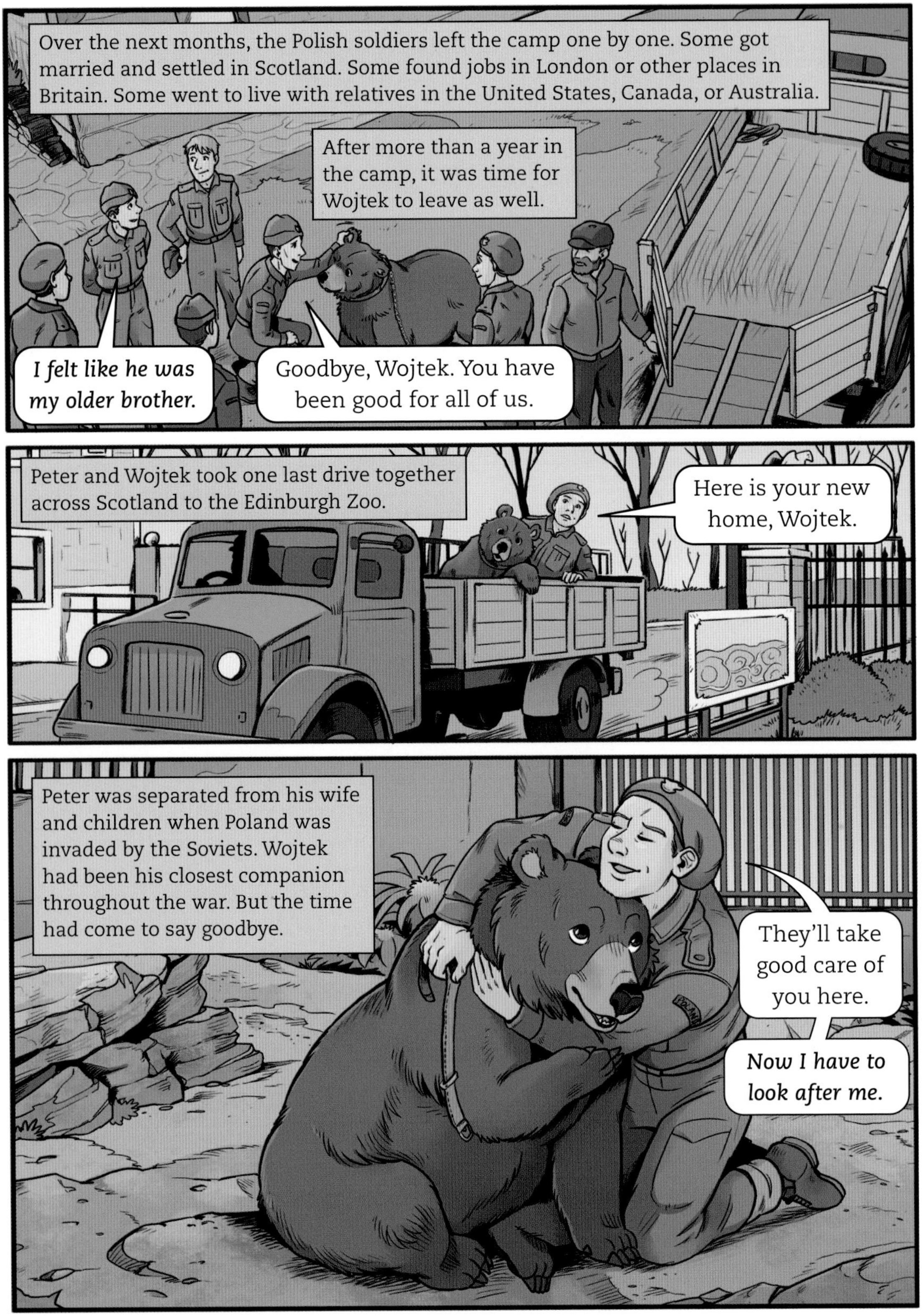
Over the next months, the Polish soldiers left the camp one by one. Some got married and settled in Scotland. Some found jobs in London or other places in Britain. Some went to live with relatives in the United States, Canada, or Australia.
After more than a year in the camp, it was time for Wojtek to leave as well.
I felt like he was my older brother.
Goodbye, Wojtek. You have been good for all of us.
Peter and Wojtek took one last drive together across Scotland to the Edinburgh Zoo.
Here is your new home, Wojtek.
Peter was separated from his wife and children when Poland was invaded by the Soviets. Wojtek had been his closest companion throughout the war. But the time had come to say goodbye.
They'll take good care of you here.
Now I have to look after me.

A Hero Remembered

Wojtek was a Syrian brown bear. He grew to stand almost 6 feet (1.8 meters) tall when he stood on his back legs. By the end of his life, he weighed 1,100 pounds (500 kilograms).

Along with earning the rank of Corporal, Wojtek also inspired the official logo of the Polish 22nd Artillery Supply Company—a bear carrying an artillery shell.

Wojtek lived 16 years in the Edinburgh Zoo. He was one of the most popular animals at the zoo, and sometimes even appeared on children's TV shows. Over the years, several Polish soldiers who were living in Britain came to visit him. Wojtek died in 1963 at age 21.

Today, statues of Wojtek are found in Edinburgh, Scotland, and London, England. Several cities in Poland also have statues of the heroic bear. Another statue stands in Cassino, Italy, where the bear helped his friends in the Polish 22nd Artillery Supply Company fight against the Nazis.

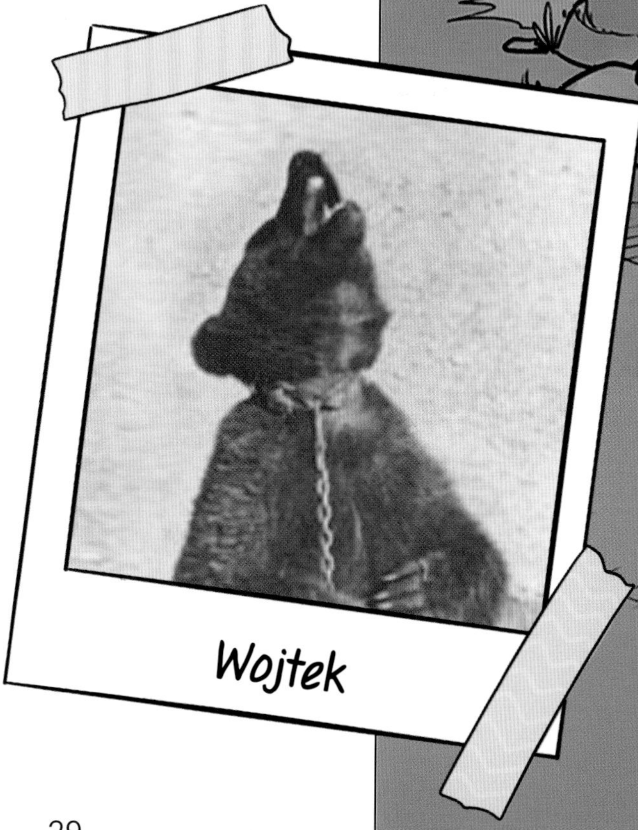
Wojtek

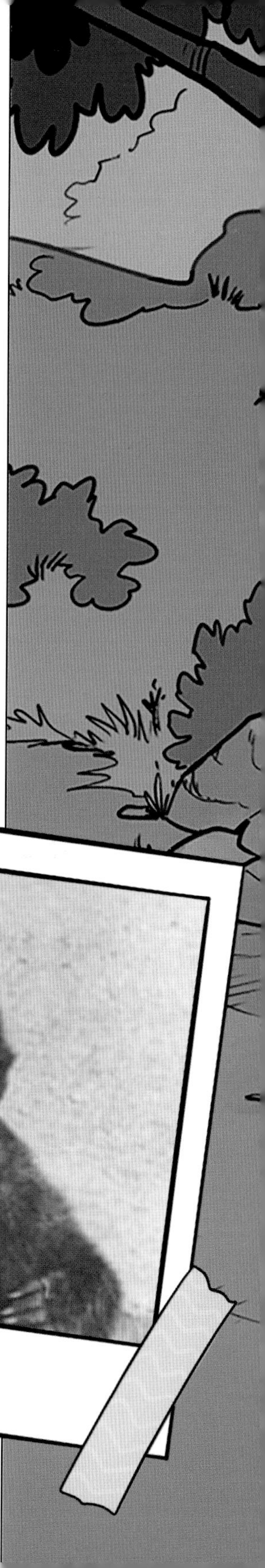

Glossary

ammunition depot
(am-yuh-NI-shuhn DEE-poh)
a place where weapons,
bullets, and shells are stored
for the military to use

artillery (ar-TIL-uh-ree)
cannons and other large
guns used to fire shells at
enemy positions in battle

barrage (buh-RAHJ)
heavy gunfire

deplete (dih-PLEET)
to seriously decrease
the size or amount of
something

invade (in-VADE)
to send armed forces into
another country to take
it over

liberate (LIB-uh-reyt)
to free a nation or area
from control by a foreign
or unjust government

mascot (MAS-kot)
a person or animal that
represents a group as a symbol

monastery
(MAHN-uh-ster-ee)
a building or buildings
where monks live and work

morale (muh-RAL)
the mental or emotional
condition of a person or
group of people

peninsula
(puh-NIN-suh-luh)
a piece of land that is
surrounded by water on
three sides

surrender (suh-REN-dur)
to give up or admit defeat

trek (TREK)
a slow or difficult journey,
usually over a long distance

venom (VEN-uhm)
poisonous liquid produced
by some animals